••• Sue Elliott and Liz Gallivan

Preliminary for Schools TRAINER

SIX PRACTICE TESTS
WITHOUT ANSWERS

CAMBRIDGE
UNIVERSITY PRESS

University Printing House, Cambridge CB2 8BS, United Kingdom

Cambridge University Press is part of the University of Cambridge.

It furthers the University's mission by disseminating knowledge in the pursuit of education, learning and research at the highest international levels of excellence.

www.cambridge.org
Information on this title: www.cambridge.org/9780521174855

© Cambridge University Press 2012

This publication is in copyright. Subject to statutory exception and to the provisions of relevant collective licensing agreements, no reproduction of any part may take place without the written permission of Cambridge University Press.

First published 2012
23rd printing 2016

Printed in Dubai by Oriental Press

A catalogue record for this publication is available from the British Library

ISBN 978-0-521-17485-5 Practice Tests without answers
ISBN 978-0-521-17487-9 Practice Tests with answers and Audio CDs
ISBN 978-0-521-17486-2 Audio CDs (3)

Cambridge University Press has no responsibility for the persistence or accuracy of URLs for external or third-party internet websites referred to in this publication, and does not guarantee that any content on such websites is, or will remain, accurate or appropriate. Information regarding prices, travel timetables and other factual information given in this work is correct at the time of first printing but Cambridge University Press does not guarantee the accuracy of such information thereafter.

It is normally necessary for written permission for copying to be obtained in advance from a publisher. The answer sheets at the back of this book are designed to be copied and distributed in class. The normal requirements are waived here and it is not necessary to write to Cambridge University Press for permission for an individual teacher to make copies for use within his or her own classroom. Only those pages which carry the wording '© UCLES 2011 Photocopiable' may be copied.

Contents

Introduction		4

Training and Exam Practice

Test 1	Paper 1 Reading & Writing	10
	Paper 2 Listening	34
	Paper 3 Speaking	44
Test 2	Paper 1 Reading & Writing	52
	Paper 2 Listening	76
	Paper 3 Speaking	86

Practice Tests

Test 3	Paper 1 Reading & Writing	94
	Paper 2 Listening	106
	Paper 3 Speaking	111
Test 4	Paper 1 Reading & Writing	112
	Paper 2 Listening	124
	Paper 3 Speaking	129
Test 5	Paper 1 Reading & Writing	130
	Paper 2 Listening	142
	Paper 3 Speaking	147
Test 6	Paper 1 Reading & Writing	148
	Paper 2 Listening	160
	Paper 3 Speaking	165

Sample Answer Sheets	166
Acknowledgements	171
Speaking Part 2 Images	C1
Speaking Part 3 Photographs	C7
Additional Photographs	C13

Introduction

If you are aged between 11 and 15 and want to take **PET for Schools**, this book is for you!

This book is called '**Trainer**' because it is full of exercises to help you get better and better at doing each part of **PET for Schools**.

So, complete all the exercises then do all the practice papers! If you train and work hard, you'll soon be ready to take **PET for Schools**.

First, do the grammar and vocabulary exercises on each **Training** page. Then do the task on the **Exam practice** page and check your answers.

On Training pages you will find:

 Cambridge Learner Corpus

This shows information about mistakes that some **PET** candidates make. If you do these useful exercises, you will learn not to make these mistakes when you do **PET for Schools**.

Tips!

These are ideas to help you do well in the exam. For example: *To find the answers in Reading Part 2 you need to paraphrase.*

Remember!

These are quick reminders about grammar points or vocabulary that you should learn. For example: *When a verb follows a preposition or verbs of liking* (like, love, dislike, hate) *the verb usually takes the –ing form.*

On Exam practice pages you will find:

- a **PET for Schools exam task** for you to try and complete
- **advice** to help you with different parts of the task.

Tests 3, 4, 5 and 6:

When you finish Tests 1 and 2 you will be ready to do complete **PET for Schools practice tests**.

Tests 3, 4, 5 and 6 are just like real **PET for Schools** Reading and Writing, Listening and Speaking papers. Doing these tests will give you extra help to prepare for the exam.

Keep a record of your scores as you do the tests. You may find that your scores are good in some parts of the test but you may need to practise other parts more. Make simple tables like this to help record your scores.

Paper 1 Reading

	Part 1	Part 2	Part 3	Part 4	Part 5
Test 3					
Test 4					
Test 5					
Test 6					

Other features of the PET for Schools Trainer

- **Visual material**

In the Speaking Test the examiner will give you a booklet with pictures and photographs in it. The visual material in the colour section from pages C1–C16 will help you practise and become familiar with the type of pictures and photographs you will see in the test and help you increase your confidence.

- **Answer sheets**

Look at these to see what the PET for Schools answer sheets in the test look like and learn how to complete them. Ask your teacher to photocopy them so that you can use them when you do your practice tests.

- **Two audio CDs**

Listen to these to practise the Listening paper. You will need to listen to these to practise some parts of the Speaking paper too.

The Preliminary English Test for Schools

Contents
PET for Schools has three papers:

Reading and Writing: 1 hour 30 minutes
There are five parts to the Reading test and you will need to be able to read and understand a range of texts from short notices and messages to longer articles from brochures, magazines and newspapers. You will also have to choose the correct words to complete a text.
In the three parts of the Writing test you will have to rewrite sentences and be able to produce both a short message (between 35–45 words long) and a longer piece of writing (a letter or a story about 100 words long).

Listening: 30 minutes
In the four parts of the Listening paper you will need to be able to listen and understand people who are talking together and people who are giving information about something. You will have to choose or write the answers to the questions which are about what these people say. Don't worry! The people talk about everyday topics, speak clearly and don't talk too fast.

Speaking: 10–12 minutes
You will need to be able to listen and understand what the examiner is saying. You will have to answer some questions about yourself. You will be given some pictures and photographs to look at and you will ask and answer questions about the pictures with another candidate. You will also need to speak on your own about a photograph. Then in the final part you will speak with the other candidate again. Usually candidates take the Speaking Test with just one other candidate but sometimes candidates take the Speaking Test in groups of three.

Frequently asked questions:

What level is PET for Schools?

PET for Schools is Council of Europe Level B1. At B1 level PET students can:
- understand the main points of straightforward instructions or public announcements
- understand instructions on classes and homework given by a teacher
- understand factual articles in magazines and letters from friends expressing personal opinions
- understand most information of a factual nature in his/her school subjects
- ask simple questions and take part in factual conversations in school
- talk about things such as films and music and describe his/her reactions to them
- write letters or make notes on familiar or predictable matters
- take basic notes in a lesson
- write a description of an event, for example a school trip.

For more information on 'Can Do' statements go to:
http://www.cambridgeesol.org/exams/exams-info/cefr.html

Note that different students have different strengths and weaknesses. Some may be good at speaking but not so good at writing; others may be good at reading but not so good at listening. The B1 Level 'Can Do' statements simply help teachers understand what PET for Schools candidates should generally be able to do at this level.

What grade do I need to pass PET for Schools?

There are two passing grades for PET for Schools: Pass with Merit and Pass. Candidates who don't get a passing grade but show that they have ability in English at a slightly lower level (Council of Europe Level A2) get level A2 on their certificate. Candidates who score below level A2 get a fail grade.

Basic user		Independent user		Proficient user	
A1	A2	B1	B2	C1	C2
	Key for Schools (KET for Schools)	Preliminary for Schools (PET for Schools)	First for Schools (FCE for Schools)		

What marks do I need to pass each paper, and to pass the exam?

Candidates do not have to get a certain mark to pass each paper in the test. The final mark for PET for Schools is the total number of marks from all three papers: Reading and Writing, Listening and Speaking. There are an equal number of possible marks for reading, writing, listening and speaking in PET for Schools.

How can I find out about my performance in each paper of PET for Schools?

Before you get a certificate you will get a Statement of Results telling you how well you did in PET for Schools. As well as your result and your score out of 100 it also gives you your 'Candidate Profile'. This is an easy-to-read graph that shows how you performed on all the papers of the test compared to the all the other candidates taking the same test. If you do not get the score that you wanted, the Candidate Profile will show you which of the skills (reading, writing, listening or speaking) you did well in and which you need to improve.

Is PET for Schools suitable for candidates of any age?

PET for Schools is more suitable for students who are at school and aged from 11–15. To make sure that the material is interesting for this age group and not too difficult or too easy for the B1 level, all the parts of the Reading, Writing, Listening and Speaking papers are pre-tested. This means that different groups of students try the materials for each part of the test first. The material will then only be used in real exams if the results of the pre-tests show that they are suitable for candidates who want to take PET for Schools.

> Can I use pens and pencils in the exam?

In PET for Schools candidates must use **pencil** in all the papers. It's useful for you if you want to change one of your answers on the answer sheet.

> What happens if I don't have enough time to finish writing?

You can only be given marks for what you write on your answer sheet, so if you do not complete this then you will miss the chance to show the examiner what you can do and how good your English is. Watch the clock and plan your time carefully. Do not waste time writing your answers on other pieces of paper. However, in the Listening test it is a good idea to write your answers on the question paper first. You will have time at the end to move your answers from the question paper to your answer sheet.

> If I write in capital letters, will it affect my score?

No. You do not lose marks for writing in capital letters in PET for Schools. Whether you choose to use capital letters or not, you should always make sure that your handwriting is clear and easy to read. Remember that the examiners can't mark a piece of writing that they can't read!

Test 1 Training   Reading Part 1

In this part you:

- **read** five different short texts, e.g. signs, messages, labels, emails and notices
- **choose** which option (**A**, **B** or **C**) means the same as the short text

Focus Short texts

1 **We see short texts everywhere in our daily lives. Match the short texts 1–6 with the correct text type a–f.**

Tip! Look carefully at each short text. Use all the clues to work out what type of text it is: the words used, the headings and the layout.

Text types

a a note *text 5*
b a sign
c an email
d a text message
e a notice
f a label

①
DANGER
ROAD REPAIRS
AHEAD

②
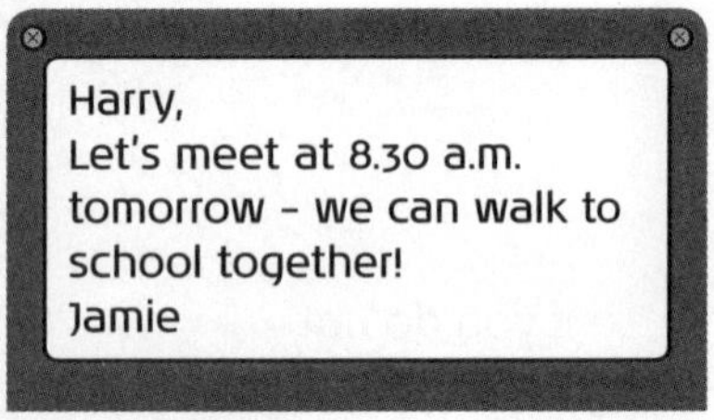
Harry,
Let's meet at 8.30 a.m. tomorrow – we can walk to school together!
Jamie

③
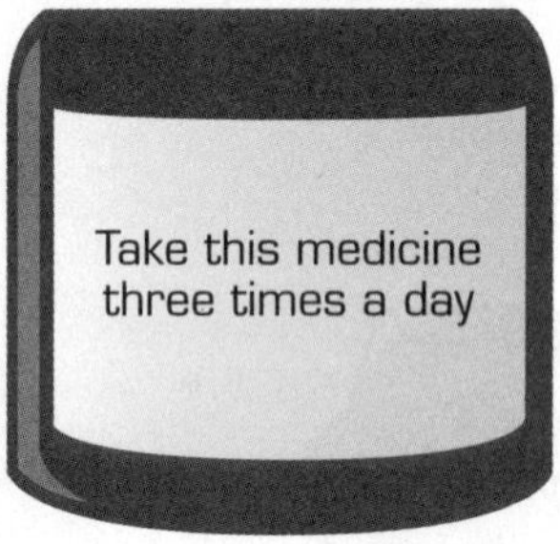
Take this medicine three times a day

④
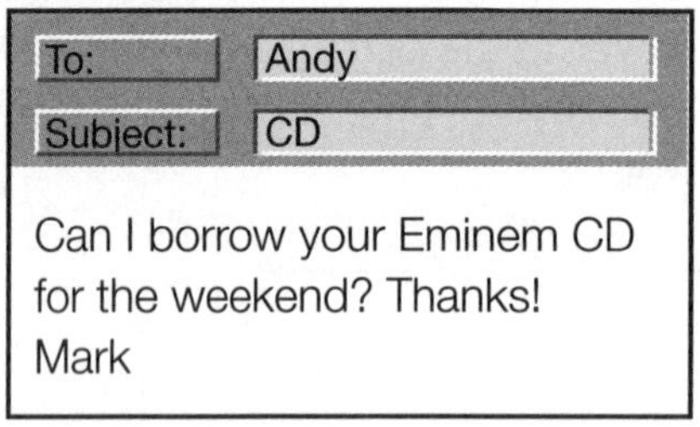
To: Andy
Subject: CD
Can I borrow your Eminem CD for the weekend? Thanks!
Mark

⑤
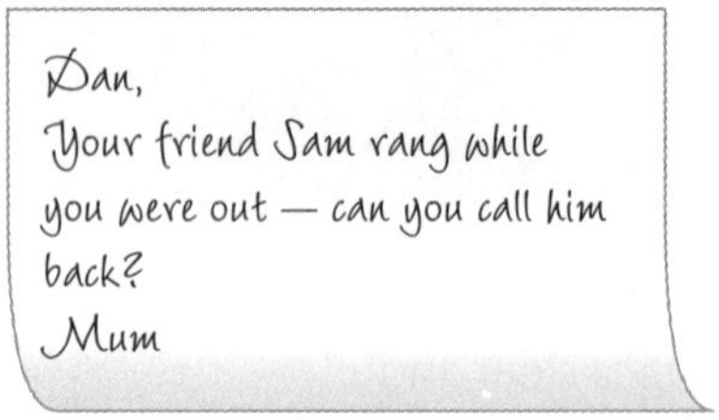
Dan,
Your friend Sam rang while you were out – can you call him back?
Mum

⑥
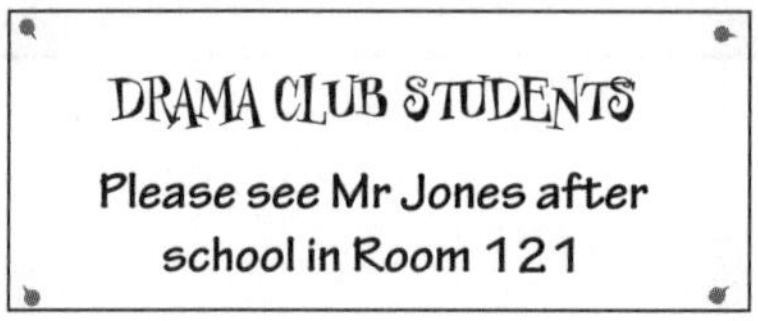
DRAMA CLUB STUDENTS
Please see Mr Jones after school in Room 121

2 **Compare your answers with a partner. Do you agree? Where might you see each text?**

Grammar Imperatives

3 Match the imperatives in bold in each sentence with where you might see them.

1 **Turn** off your mobile.
2 Cyclists – **turn** left here.
3 **Push** to open.
4 **Press** button to call lift.
5 **Heat** in microwave for 3 minutes.

a in a tall building
b on a classroom wall
c on a food packet
d in the street
e on a door

> **Tip!** Look carefully at the imperatives in Part 1 short texts to understand what they are instructing readers to do.

Focus Context

4 Match the texts with the places where you might see them (their context).

> **Tip!** Be careful – there are more places in the list than you need.

① **DO NOT WALK ON THE GRASS**

② *QUEUE HERE FOR THE 7.30 PERFORMANCE*

③ Please leave dishes on your tray after you have finished your food

④ **TRAVELLING WITHOUT A TICKET IS FORBIDDEN**

⑤  PEDESTRIANS AND CYCLISTS ONLY

⑥ TODAY ONLY
EVERYTHING HALF-PRICE!
COME IN AND HAVE A LOOK!

⑦ THIS AREA IS FOR QUIET READING AND STUDY

a outside a post office
b on a train
c outside a theatre
d at a swimming pool
e on a road
f in a shop window
g on a packet of food
h in a library
i on a medicine bottle
j in a café
k outside a doctor's surgery
l in a park

5 In pairs, talk about the places you didn't use in exercise 4. Write a sign for each place and ask your partner to guess the place.

Test 1 Exam practice Reading • Part 1

Questions 1 – 5

Look at the text in each question.
What does it say?
Mark the correct letter **A**, **B** or **C** on your answer sheet.

Tip! Look carefully at each option – A, B or C – before making your choice. Your answer must match with what the short text says.

Example:

0

> Hi Jon. Your friend Mark came to the house earlier to see if you were in. Can you ring him back before 5.30 tonight? He's going to football practice then.
> Mum

Mum is texting Jon to

A   tell him to contact his friend.

B   remind him that it's football practice tonight.

C   ask if he'll be home before 5.30.

Answer:

1

> AFTER-SCHOOL MUSIC LESSONS
> BEGINNING AGAIN TONIGHT!
> FIRST CLASS IN ROOM 452 –
> COME ALONG!

A   There are first-class music lessons in Room 452 tonight after school.

B   If you want to begin music lessons after school, go to Room 452 tonight.

C   To be the first to attend music classes in school, go to Room 452.

2

> To: Mr Smith's students
> Subject: Film club
>
> This Friday, Film Club is showing the English film *Highway*, based on the book we are studying this term. It's free – just turn up early to get a seat!

A   Students should book to see *Highway* at Film Club on Friday.

B   You won't get into Film Club on Friday unless you take some money.

C   If you're in Mr Smith's class, it's a good idea to attend Film Club on Friday.

Advice

1 first class = the first class of the term

3

Hi Jake,
I've just read some of the book Ben lent me. He couldn't put it down but I didn't finish it – I lost interest. Have you read it?
Sam

Sam is contacting Jake to

A   say he disagreed with Ben's opinion about the book.

B   ask what he thought of Ben's book.

C   tell him how good Ben's book was.

4

Michaela
John's party starts at 6 tonight, so Dad and I will pick you up at 5.30.
Be ready!
Shaz

Shaz is texting Michaela to

A   ask her for a lift to the party.

B   explain the travel arrangements to the party.

C   tell her what time she'll see her at the party.

5

LAKESIDE POOL

NON-SWIMMERS SHOULD STAY IN THE SHALLOW END WHILE WAVE MACHINE IS OPERATING

While the wave machine is working

A   people who can't swim should leave the water.

B   people should go to shallow water to enjoy the waves.

C   people shouldn't go into deeper water if they can't swim.

Advice

3 Who is writing to whom? What about? Did Sam enjoy the book? What about Ben? Has Jake read the book yet?

Test 1 Training — Reading Part 2

In this part you:

- **read**   five descriptions of people and eight short texts on a variety of subjects
- **match**   what each person requires with information in one of the eight texts

Focus Reading for detail

1. Maria is looking for an e-friend. Read her email, then close your book and try to remember as much information as you can about her.

   From: Maria

   Hi! My name is Maria, and I'd like to send my e-friend emails and letters through the post and get some back! I love going to the pool in my town, and I enjoy other sports too, but I find shopping a bit boring. I create a lot of my own cartoons, but I'm not very good at it, so I'd like to write to someone who is!

2. Look at the emails below from two girls called Katie and Jennie. Underline information in the two texts which matches with information about Maria.

   Tip! Read and underline the key facts about each person before you read the eight short texts.

   From: Katie

   Hi! I'm **Katie** and I spend a lot of my free time in the town centre with my friends, buying clothes. I'm also in my school's swimming and basketball teams, and I draw a lot of cartoons – I want to send some of them to be published in the school magazine, but my teacher says I need more practice first. I check my email and reply every day, but I'm not good at writing letters, I'm afraid!

   Remember!
   Knowing about **synonyms** (words that mean the same thing) and **word families** can help in Part 2, e.g. watersports: *swimming, going to the pool, sailing, windsurfing.*

   From: Jennie

   Hello! I'm called **Jennie**, and my hobby is making cartoons out of my own artwork – I've already had some of them published in a teenage magazine! I love sending long letters to friends, and I email a lot. I spend the rest of my spare time doing different watersports, which I really love. A lot of my friends go to the shopping mall every Saturday but I'm too busy for that – and I'm not keen on it, anyway.

3. Which girl would Maria be more interested in writing to – Katie or Jennie? Why? Compare the information you underlined with a partner.

4. What kind of person would you look for as an e-friend? What kind of things would you say about yourself? Compare your ideas with a partner.

Test 1 Exam practice — Reading • Part 2

Questions 6 – 10

The people below all want to find a place to go for a skiing holiday. On the next page there are reviews of eight ski centres. Decide which centre would be the most suitable for the following people to go to.

For questions **6–10**, mark the correct letter **(A–H)** on your answer sheet.

Tip! Try to remember as much as you can about each person's description before you start looking for a matching text. This can save you time.

6  Maria's an intermediate-level skier who wants individual lessons, at a reasonable price, to get to advanced level. Maria and her family want somewhere peaceful, with a cinema to go to in the evenings.

7  Dan and his family want somewhere that's not crowded, so they don't spend time waiting for ski lifts. Dan's a beginner and wants classes with other teenagers. He'd like to do other sports, too.

8  Jane and her brother want to improve their advanced skiing techniques, and have classes in other snow sports. Jane loves animals, and she'd like to see some during her holiday.

9  Karl's family are good skiers, and want somewhere with a guide to take them off skiing through the mountains. Karl wants to stay somewhere with great food, where he can also swim.

10  Tadeusz and his 12-year-old brother are beginners. They want to travel to the ski slopes together without their parents, and ski in the same class. They'd like a lively ski centre near a town.

Advice

*6 Which two centres offer individual lessons at a reasonable price? Which one of these offers a cinema? What's another word for **peaceful**? And why is D no good for Maria?*

7 Which centres offer other sports? Dan and his family don't want somewhere crowded or to wait for ski lifts – so why are B and H no good?

Eight Ski Centres

A Eadensberg

This centre's good for skiers of all abilities, with reasonably-priced lessons for individuals wishing to improve quickly. Be prepared to wait at the lifts, though! It's some distance from the town, too, so there's little evening entertainment – but there are classes in ice skating, snowboarding and swimming.

B Nansville

This ski centre offers separate classes for teenagers and children, and has instructors trained to ski cross-country with groups – apart from beginners! Several hotels offer good cooking and indoor pools, and there's also a skateboard park and children's zoo. Under-18s must be accompanied on lifts, which are sometimes crowded.

C Chambrix

Learn to ski for the first time – and make fast progress at any level. Young people's group lessons are for mixed ages, and there are low-cost one-to-one lessons too. When skiing's finished, there are great restaurants, and a multi-screen movie theatre! Apart from these, the centre's rather quiet, and some distance from town.

D St Barone

The hotels in this quiet centre have ski lifts right outside, so no problems getting to the slopes – and no queues! The centre has good classes for teenagers to ski together, up to intermediate level, although one-to-one lessons are costly. For the evenings there are fantastic restaurants and a great cinema.

E Zeelunds

The hotels here have lifts that quickly take you to the slopes. There are group classes for teenagers, although slopes are not challenging enough for advanced skiers. Transport to the town can be difficult, but try the activities on offer in the centre – skateboarding, swimming, cinema or ice skating.

F Palanta

This busy centre is close to town, with its cinemas, shops and internet cafés. Younger skiers are taught in groups of any age up to intermediate level, so teenage family members can ski together. And there's a minibus to collect young skiers from hotels and take them safely to ski lessons without mum or dad!

G Davrano

This small centre's great for all serious skiers. There are also experienced guides who'll take groups or individuals off the marked slopes to ski through the mountains – if your skiing's good enough! Or why not try the centre's wildlife-watching trips? The centre's also well known for its fantastic restaurants, but there's little other entertainment.

H Morland

Adults, teenagers and younger children have their own groups or one-to-one classes here whatever their level, although parents must accompany under-18s on lifts – go early to avoid crowds! There's instruction in snowboarding and skating, too. And in the evenings take a horse-riding trip through the snow!

Test 1 Training — Reading Part 3

In this part you:
- **read**   a text based on fact
- **decide**   if statements about the text are correct or incorrect

Grammar   Present and past simple passive

1   Circle the correct passive form in each sentence.
1. School uniform *is worn / are worn* by all the pupils on Sports Day.
2. Our sports clothes *is kept / are kept* in our lockers.
3. We *isn't allowed / aren't allowed* to wear jeans on Sports Day.
4. Parents *is always invited / are always invited* to come and watch Sports Day.
5. My sports prize *is displayed / are displayed* in the living room!
6. Sport *is chosen / are chosen* by a lot of pupils as their favourite after-school activity.

> **Tip!** Understanding the meaning of sentences in Part 3 may depend on understanding grammar such as the passive.

> **Remember!** We use the passive when the action or event is more important than who did it.
> *Students **are requested** to leave mobile phones at home.* We don't need to know who does the action.
> *The library **is being painted** this week.* (= Somebody is painting the library this week.)

2   Complete the second sentence to make the passive form of the first sentence.
1. Our history teacher <u>gave</u> us a lot of homework last week.
   We .... a lot of homework by our history teacher last week.
2. Our maths teacher <u>didn't ask</u> us to hand in our work today.
   We .... to hand in our work by our maths teacher today.
3. My brother and I didn't feel well at school yesterday, so our dad <u>collected</u> us.
   My brother and I .... from school by our dad yesterday.
4. I <u>took</u> this photo as part of a project for art.
   This photo .... as part of a project for art.
5. My class <u>grew</u> these tomatoes in the school garden.
   These tomatoes .... in the school garden.
6. Mr Smith is a new teacher – he <u>didn't teach</u> me last year.
   I .... by Mr Smith last year.

Focus   Reading for meaning

3   Tick (✔) the sentence (a or b) with the same meaning as the first sentence.

> **Tip!** It's important to identify phrases and sentences that have the same meaning.

Example   I enjoy science more than any other lesson at school.
    a Science is my favourite class. ✔   **b** I like all my lessons at school, including science.

1. I wish I could wear my own clothes at school, instead of my uniform.
   - **a** I really hate my school uniform.
   - **b** I'd prefer not to wear my uniform to school.
2. I have no idea at all how to do this homework.
   - **a** This homework is giving me no problem at all.
   - **b** I need some help with this homework.
3. I won't get you a ticket for the school concert unless you call by six o'clock.
   - **a** Phone me before six if you want me to get you a ticket.
   - **b** If I don't hear from you by six, I'll get you a ticket.
4. Everyone missed the programme except Jack.
   - **a** Everyone apart from Jack watched the programme.
   - **b** Jack was the only one who watched the programme.

Test 1 Exam practice — Reading • Part 3

Questions 11 – 20

Look at the sentences below about a visit to a school by a robot.
Read the text on the opposite page to decide if each sentence is correct or incorrect.
If it is correct, mark **A** on your answer sheet.
If it is not correct, mark **B** on your answer sheet.

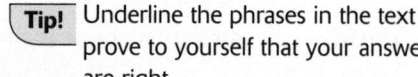 **Tip!** Underline the phrases in the text to prove to yourself that your answers are right.

11 Jake says that people at the school he attends enjoy studying science.

12 Visitors from outside Jake's school often talk to the students during Science Days.

13 Jake and his classmates were told in advance that a robot was coming to the school.

14 Jake and his classmates were surprised at the actions that Gizmo the robot could perform.

15 The robot was developed very quickly by the company that created him.

16 Jake's classmates thought that Gizmo was very polite.

17 The robot looked as if it realised when there was someone in front of it.

18 Jake and his classmates were able to have a discussion with Gizmo.

19 Jake's headmaster felt that the day achieved what he had hoped.

20 Jake now wants to own a robot exactly like Gizmo.

Advice

11 What does Jake say about 'people my age' and people at the school he attends?

13 Did the students know what was planned for them on the last Science Day?

15 How long did it take the company to develop Gizmo?

A SPECIAL VISITOR

By Jake Matthews, aged 14

I know some people my age don't really like doing science at school. But I go to a big high school where science subjects are really popular amongst the students. We frequently have special days called Science Days at the school, which are organised by our headmaster and all the teachers. On these days, people working in science are invited to come and tell us about their jobs. On the last Science Day we had no idea what was planned for us – but a real working robot came to spend the day with us at school! It was fantastic!

The robot's name was Gizmo. We were told he was one of the most advanced robots in the world, and we quickly realised he was no ordinary machine. He could do lots of amazing things like walking up and down stairs, waving and even dancing to rock music! He was about the same size as us, with long arms and legs, but apart from that not at all similar to a real person – instead of a face, for example, he had a helmet like a spaceman's. It was very exciting to come face to face with the latest technology!

The company that Gizmo belongs to said it actually took them as long as 20 years to make him, but they think that within another 20 years, he will be as common a sight in homes as a microwave oven. Everyone at my school liked the way Gizmo behaved, as he always said *please* and *thank you*, and even fetched our drinks and snacks! He also seemed to know that he needed to stop when one of the students walked in front of him.

The funny thing about Gizmo, though, was that he could do so many things, but when we tried to make conversation with him, he didn't say anything at all. The company that developed the robot hope they can make one that will do complicated things like having discussions, but they think it's some years away.

The whole day with Gizmo was a success. Now lots of us feel we want to go into careers in science and technology – which was just the result our headmaster had wanted. He said the day had been worth all the hard work to arrange it. As for me, I want to become a scientist and learn to make a robot – even better than the one that paid a visit to my school!

Test 1 Training — Reading Part 4

In this part you:
- **read** a short text that includes opinions and feelings
- **choose** a correct answer (**A**, **B**, **C** or **D**) from five multiple-choice questions

Vocabulary Understanding adjectives

1 Write the adjectives under the correct heading.

> surprised   angry   disappointed   afraid   nervous
> satisfied   worried   excited   tired   embarrassed   guilty
> jealous   bored   confident   cheerful

Tip! In Part 4 you may need to understand adjectives that describe what the writer thinks or feels.

Positive feelings	Negative feelings

2 Use adjectives from exercise 1 to describe how each speaker below feels.

Example   I thought I was late for the bus, so I didn't expect to see it still at the bus stop!   *surprised*

1 I've had sports all day at school today – so I'm going to bed as soon as I get home!
2 I can't wait until it's time for my birthday party!
3 I thought our team would win the beach football match – but we lost, sadly.
4 When I was in a crowded shop yesterday, a boy stood on my foot – and didn't apologise!
5 I saw my new friend in town yesterday – but I completely forgot her name!
6 This film isn't very interesting – I keep thinking of something else.
7 I've trained really hard for the race tomorrow – I know I'll do OK!
8 Oh dear! I'm sure I put my purse in my bag – and now it's not there!

3 Choose three adjectives from exercise 1 that you didn't use in exercise 2. Write three sentences describing situations where you might feel like this.

1 ....
2 ....
3 ....

Grammar -ing forms and infinitive with to

4 Complete each sentence with the correct form of the verbs in brackets.

Example   My brother isn't keen on ...**eating**.... (eat) a lot of ice cream – it makes him feel cold!

> **Remember!**
> When a verb follows a preposition or verbs of liking (*like, love, dislike, hate*), the verb usually takes the *-ing* form, e.g. *I like **going** swimming. I'm interested in **learning** to play chess.* But don't forget to use the infinitive with *will, can, must, should*, etc., e.g. *I would like **to go** into town.*

1 I'd hate .... (go) somewhere really far away for my holiday.
2 I really dislike .... (walk) round museums for hours – it's boring!
3 Would you prefer .... (go) on holiday in the mountains or by the sea?
4 Would you mind .... (look after) my pet fish while we're away?
5 I'm really good at .... (take) photos of all the places we visit.
6 I'm not very interested in .... (do) the same things as my brother all the time.
7 We're all looking forward to .... (see) our family again when we get home.
8 It's raining, so don't forget .... (take) your umbrella with you.

5 Match the sentence halves.

1 When we travel long distances, I really enjoy
2 We're going to the seaside, because we all want
3 If it's raining tomorrow, I don't mind
4 When the holiday is over, I really hate
5 For our next family climbing holiday, I'd love
6 Would you like

a unpacking all my bags at home!
b going to a museum instead of the zoo.
c to come with us on our next holiday?
d going by train, rather than by plane.
e to swim every day!
f to go to some really high mountains.

👁 PET candidates often make mistakes with *-ing* forms and the infinitive.

6 Cross out and correct the mistake in each sentence.

Example   I'd like ~~going~~ to the swimming pool with your brother and you.   .....**to go**.....

1 If you are interested in **to visit** historic buildings, I think you should go to Rome.   ....
2 I'd prefer **going** on Saturday if that's OK.   ....
3 I wanted **coming** to the party, but I have an exam tomorrow.   ....
4 I am looking forward **to see** you next Saturday.   ....
5 I would like you **sending** me a photo of your family.   ....

Test 1 Exam practice — Reading • Part 4

Questions 21 – 25

Read the text and questions below.
For each question, mark the correct letter **A**, **B**, **C** or **D** on your answer sheet.

Tip! Read through the questions first so that you understand the context.

Ed Gardner – Airline Pilot

At 20, Ed Gardner is too young to drive a bus in some countries. Yet he regularly flies tourists to their holiday destinations.

Ed started flying at 14 – you can't be any younger than that – before he could even drive a car. He flew unaccompanied at 16, and got his private pilot's licence on his 17th birthday. His dad's an airline pilot too, and Ed has flown with him on passenger flights since Ed became a pilot. 'He never pushed me to become a pilot, but as soon as I said I wanted to do it, he was pleased. And Dad gave me money for my training, and now I'm paying him back. He's been very helpful.'

After training, he immediately started work as a pilot for a commercial airline. The captain is the boss, but Ed's allowed to do almost the same work apart from operating the plane on the runway at the airport. When Ed first joined the airline he flew mail to different places. Then he changed to passenger flights. 'I was excited, but you don't really get to talk to the passengers. The captain is in charge, but if they fly out on a short trip, you fly the plane back, for example.'

There are other pilots around Ed's age, but they are a bit older because they've done something else before they came to flying. But it's not everyone that can get a job so soon. Ed, who now flies regularly to Europe and Africa, says simply, 'I think I just came along at the right time!'

21 What is Ed Gardner trying to do in the text?
   A explain why pilots should start training early for their careers
   B tell readers why he chose to be a pilot
   C describe the work involved in becoming a pilot
   D discuss whether teenagers should be allowed to fly planes

> **Advice**
>
> *22 What did Ed's dad allow him to do that helped him?*
>
> *23 What did Ed look forward to doing? Did he get to do that? So how might he feel?*

22 Ed's father, who is also a pilot, helped Ed by
   A agreeing to fly with him on some passenger flights.
   B offering to pay for all of his training.
   C encouraging him to choose the right career for him.
   D letting him improve his skills in his small plane.

23 As a pilot, Ed was disappointed at first that
   A he couldn't do everything the captain did on the plane.
   B he had very little contact with his passengers.
   C he sometimes got no time off before return flights.
   D he was asked to transport mail instead of people.

24 What does Ed say about his achievements at such a young age?
   A He feels he's been lucky to join a company very quickly.
   B He thinks what he's done may be very unusual.
   C He's very proud of the position he's got to.
   D He wishes he'd tried something else before he started flying.

25 What would Ed write in an email to an old schoolfriend?

   A I last saw you at my party on my 17th birthday – sorry it finished early, but I was getting my pilot's licence the next day.

   B I used to travel miles to my first flying lessons, didn't I? Luckily I'd got my driving licence by then.

   C I've checked the flight you're on tomorrow – and I'll be one of your pilots! Hope you enjoy it!

   D Mum was worried when I flew on my own for the first time – she even tried to convince me not to go.

Reading Part 4

Test 1 Training — Reading Part 5

In this part you:
- **read** a text with ten spaces in it
- **choose** the correct word for each space from four options

Grammar Focus on prepositions

1 Complete the information about Mark and his plans for the weekend with prepositions from the box.

on   with   about (x2)   of   to (x2)   in   at (x2)   for

I attend school in my capital city, and I really like it. I'm quite good (0) ...*at*... history and I'm really interested (1) .... science. I'm not great (2) .... drawing, though. I showed my picture of a robot to my little sister, and she was afraid (3) .... it! There's an after-school art club at my school, but I don't know much (4) .... it. I might join, though. I've just talked (5) .... my friends (6) .... our plans for the weekend. We can't decide what to do – it depends (7) .... the weather, really. We get fed up (8) .... doing the same thing every Saturday, so this weekend we're looking (9) .... something different! I'm really looking forward (10) .... it.

Tip! In Part 5, first read all the text, then look carefully at the words before or after the spaces to complete them.

Remember! When a verb follows the preposition, it takes the *-ing* form, e.g. *I'm good at swimming*.

👁 PET candidates often make mistakes with prepositions in time expressions.

2 Complete the sentences with the correct preposition *in*, *on* or *at*.

1 Our next school holiday is .... December. We break up .... Monday 18th.
2 I often watch TV .... the weekend if it's cold. I don't usually go out .... night.
3 My favourite programme is .... 6 o'clock .... Tuesdays.

Remember! **in** September, **on** 26th September, **on** Tuesday, last/next Tuesday (no preposition), **at** 3 p.m., **in** winter, **in** the morning, **in** the afternoon, **in** the evening, **at** night, **at** the weekend

👁 PET candidates often make mistakes when using *for*, *since*, *from*, *while*, *until* and *during*.

3 Cross out the wrong word in each sentence below.

Example   I've been studying English **for** / *since* I was 11.

1 My mobile rang *while* / *during* I was sitting on the bus.
2 I have to wait *while* / *until* my birthday to open my presents.
3 We looked at lots of objects *from* / *since* the 19th century.
4 I went out on my bike several times *during* / *from* the weekend.
5 It usually snows in my country *throughout* / *from* the whole winter.
6 I haven't been to the seaside *since* / *for* several months – it's been too cold.

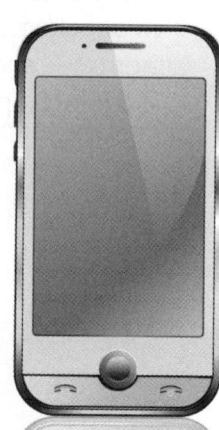

○ PET candidates often make mistakes with the words at the beginning of a sentence.

4 Circle the correct word in each sentence.
1 *Although / Despite* John's help, Ben still couldn't operate the camera.
2 *So / Because* that I don't forget my books, I've put them on the hall table.
3 *Although / Because* it was raining, Sarah stayed at home.
4 *Unless / If* Jamie rings, tell him I'll be back soon.
5 *Because / Although* he's a friend, I'm going to help him.
6 *Despite / If* Karen's there tonight, I'll ask her.

Tip! If there's a space at the beginning of the sentence in Part 5, read the whole sentence carefully to make sure you really understand what it means.

Test 1 Exam practice — Reading • Part 5

Questions 26 – 35

Read the text below and choose the correct word for each space. For each question, mark the correct letter **A**, **B**, **C** or **D** on your answer sheet.

Tip! Read through the whole text first. Try each option in the gap. Are any options impossible?

Example:

0 **A** the   **B** a   **C** one   **D** any

Answer: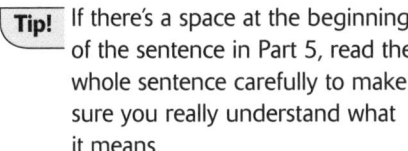

Tigers

The tiger is **(0)** .... largest member of the big cat family, and lives in parts of Asia. Most people would **(26)** .... that tigers are extremely beautiful animals, with their black and orange coats.

(27) .... tigers can't run fast for long **(28)** ...., they are good at hunting. Tigers are able to **(29)** .... high speeds, and the animals that they catch for food can often be much bigger than they **(30)** .... However, tigers behave differently from animals like lions. They will **(31)** .... their food with other tigers, even though they have gone miles to look **(32)** .... it.

The population of tigers in the world has decreased **(33)** .... the start of the 20th century, but by using radio collars, scientists have now **(34)** .... up projects that are much more **(35)** .... at finding out about how tigers live.

26	**A** tell	**B** agree	**C** decide	**D** suppose
27	**A** If	**B** Although	**C** Because	**D** So
28	**A** times	**B** moments	**C** periods	**D** ages
29	**A** reach	**B** get	**C** make	**D** go
30	**A** do	**B** will	**C** have	**D** are
31	**A** divide	**B** choose	**C** share	**D** use
32	**A** after	**B** at	**C** around	**D** for
33	**A** throughout	**B** from	**C** since	**D** during
34	**A** set	**B** given	**C** turned	**D** put
35	**A** useful	**B** successful	**C** important	**D** suitable

Advice

26 If people have the same opinion about something, what do they do?

32 What would a tiger do? Look **at** food? Look **for** food? Look **after** food? Look **around** food?

34 This means **establish**.

Test 1 Training — Writing Part 1

In this part you:
- **read** five pairs of sentences
- **complete** the second sentence so that it means the same as the first one

Grammar Direct and indirect speech

1a 🎧 02 Listen to information about Tom and his mum, then complete the sentences in direct speech.

Example Harry asked <u>if he wanted to go</u> to the cinema.
Harry asked, '<u>Do you want to go</u> to the cinema?'

1 Tom <u>suggested meeting</u> outside the cinema.
  Tom said, 'Why .... outside the cinema?'

2 Tom asked his mum if <u>she</u> could <u>drive him</u> into town.
  Tom said, 'Mum, can .... into town?'

3 She said <u>she couldn't</u> because she was a bit busy.
  She said, '........................... because I'm a bit busy.'

4 So Tom told his mum <u>not to worry</u>.
  Tom said, '..........................., Mum.'

Tip! When you change indirect speech into direct speech, think carefully about the pronouns (*I*, *he*, *she*, etc.) and the tenses.

Remember! In direct speech, 3rd person pronouns (*he*, *she*, etc.) become 1st person pronouns (e.g. *I*, *you*).

b 🎧 03 Listen and check your answers.

2 Change some more things that Tom said into direct speech.

1 Tom said he hadn't got any money.
  Tom said, 'I .... any money.'

2 Tom said he thought he was going to be late.
  Tom said, 'I .... to be late.'

3 Tom said he didn't know the time of the film.
  Tom said, 'I .... the time of the film.'

4 Tom told Harry not to be late.
  Tom told Harry, '........................... late!'

Tip! Don't forget that the two sentences in each pair must mean the same thing.

3 Change the sentences into direct speech.

1 Tom asked Harry where the cinema was.
  Tom asked Harry, '........................... the cinema?'

2 Tom asked when the film started.
  Tom asked, '........................... the film start?'

3 Tom asked Harry if he had bought any sweets.
  Tom asked Harry, '........................... any sweets?'

4 Harry wanted to know if Tom liked chocolate.
  Harry asked, '........................... chocolate, Tom?'

Remember! With questions beginning with the words **where, who, what, when, why, how, which** we use those words in the direct and the indirect speech. *'Where's the library?'* He asked **where** the library **was**.
In *yes/no* questions we use the word **if** in the indirect speech. *'Have you got any money?'* He asked me **if** I'd got any money.

Test 1 Exam practice — Writing • Part 1

Questions 1 – 5

Here are some sentences about having an older brother.
For each question, complete the second sentence so that it means the same as the first.
Use no more than three words.
Write only the missing words on your answer sheet.

Tip! Don't try to write too many words, and spell your answer correctly.

Example:

0 My brother Sammy is three years older than me.
   I'm three years .... than my brother Sammy.

Answer: | 0 | younger |

---

1 Sammy and I both love watching action films.
   Sammy loves watching action films, and .... I.

2 Sammy's much better at sport than I am.
   I'm not .... at sport as Sammy.

3 I often go into town with Sammy when we're on holiday from school.
   I often go into town with Sammy .... the school holidays.

4 Last Saturday, Sammy asked me if I wanted to go skateboarding.
   Last Saturday, Sammy asked, '.................................. to go skateboarding?'

5 It's never boring to be out with Sammy.
   I'm never .... when I'm out with Sammy.

Advice

2 The sentence is comparing the writer and Sammy. How do we compare with **as ... as**?

4 Don't forget to change the pronoun. What will **I** become? Don't forget to change the tense. What will **wanted** become in direct speech?

Test 1 Training — Writing Part 2

In this part you:

- **write** a short note or email (35–45 words) containing three different points

Vocabulary Verbs

1 Match the verbs with a sentence that communicates the idea.

1	invite	a	I can't come because I'm on holiday then.
2	describe	b	I'm so sorry – I can't make it to the party.
3	explain	c	Why don't we go to the shops and buy something?
4	suggest	d	Would you like to come to a party?
5	thank	e	The T-shirt's red with black stripes and long sleeves.
6	apologise	f	I'm really grateful for your help.

2 Write a sentence for each of these instructions.

1 Explain to a friend what you want to buy in town on Saturday.

....

2 Apologise for being late yesterday.

....

3 Invite your friend to come to a football match.

....

4 Thank your friend for a present you received.

....

5 Suggest going swimming with your friend.

....

6 Describe what your best friend looks like.

....

> **Tip!** Practise writing short messages of 35–45 words in length. Read the question carefully and underline the key verb in the instruction.

> **Remember!**
> There are a number of different ways to suggest things:
> **Why don't we go** to the cinema?
> **How about going** to the cinema?
> **Let's go** to the cinema.
> **Shall we go** to the cinema?

3 Write four short messages and suggest these things to different friends.

| have a pizza | watch a DVD | play a computer game |
| listen to a CD | | |

> **Remember!**
> Look at these ways of opening and closing an email or message.
> Hi!   Hello …   Dear …
> See you soon.   Best wishes
> Love from …   Bye for now

👁 PET candidates often forget to include some of the points in the instructions.

4 Look at the question and three example candidate answers below. Use the checklist to decide if the candidates have written a good answer or not.

Tip! Make sure you write the correct number of words. Don't make your answer too short – or too long. The more you write, the more mistakes you can make.

You have just moved to a new house.
Write an email to your English friend, Chris. In your email you should:

- say where your new house is
- describe what the house is like
- invite Chris to visit you.

From: Candidate A

Hi Chris,

I've just moved to a new house near the town centre. It's really big and beautiful with a lovely garden. I've got a bedroom at the front so I can see the street! I think I'll really enjoy living here.

From: Candidate B

Chris,

I've just moved to a new house. My new house is in town. I'll tell you what the house is like. The house is like a small terrace house, with lots of flowers outside. I invite you to visit me!

From: Candidate C

Hello Chris,

I'm now living in a new house in the countryside! It's lovely – my parents wanted to buy it to give us more space. It's got four bedrooms, a big kitchen and a beautiful garden outside. Would you like to come and see me here? You'd really love it – you can get here easily on the train!

Best wishes,

Josh

Checklist: (tick if student has achieved the task)   Candidate A   Candidate B   Candidate C

- includes all three points
- has an opening and closing, e.g. *Dear Chris*
- uses student's own words
- is about 35–45 words

Test 1 Exam practice — Writing • Part 2

Question 6

Yesterday you went to see a film in your town. Your English friend Jo wants to know all about the film.
Write an email to Jo. In your email you should:

- tell Jo where you saw the film
- describe something exciting that happened during the film
- invite Jo to go with you to the next film you see.

Write **35–45 words** on your answer sheet.

Tip! Don't just copy the words from the question – you won't get good marks for this. Try to use your own words, if possible.

Advice

1 Underline the key words in the bullet points.

2 Remember to open and close the email correctly.

tell remember to use the past tense for this point

describe try to use some adjectives to make the film sound exciting

invite *Would you like to* + verb

Test 1 Training — Writing Part 3

In this part you:
- write   either a letter or a story using about 100 words

Grammar Linking words

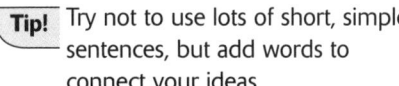 PET candidates often make mistakes when linking ideas.

1 Link the ideas in these sentences with a linking word from the box.

> so   because   as   and   although   but   despite   however

1 I like going swimming .... playing football.
2 .... I have a long journey to school, I quite like travelling there on the bus.
3 My school has a great swimming pool .... we don't use it very often.
4 I thought I was doing well in maths. ...., my teacher says I need a bit more practice.
5 I'd like to go skateboarding every day .... it's impossible during term time.
6 I went skateboarding yesterday .... the weather.

2 Complete the sentences with *so* or *because*.

1 It was snowing yesterday, ... our football match was cancelled.
2 I took my tennis racket .... I wanted to play tennis after school.
3 I don't enjoy running .... it's quite tiring!
4 My teacher's quite strict, ... we mustn't forget our football boots on sports days!

3 Cross out the wrong word(s) in each sentence.

1 *In spite of / Although* my favourite shop is out of town, it's worth the trip.
2 I go there *so / because* it's one of the biggest shops in the area.
3 The shop isn't too expensive *and / although* I like the clothes they sell there.
4 I don't like shopping on my own, *so / but* I often invite a friend to come with me.
5 I buy a lot of blue things *although / because* it's my favourite colour.
6 Yellow doesn't look good on me, *because / so* I never buy clothes that colour.

Tip! Try not to use lots of short, simple sentences, but add words to connect your ideas.

Remember!

Joining similar points:
At school, I most enjoy doing sports and going to after-school clubs. **What's more**, *I can use the IT room any time I want.*

Joining different, contrasting ideas:
There are over 30 pupils in my class **but** *we all know each other really well.*
Although *I get a lot of homework, I still have time to see my friends.*
In spite of / Despite *the rain yesterday, we all went outside to play football.*
My class is keen to go for a picnic. **However**, *our teacher doesn't like the idea.*

Remember!

To talk about reason and result, we use words like *so* and *because*.
Our teachers are really good, **so** *everyone enjoys their lessons.* (result)
The lessons are great **because** *the teachers make them fun.* (reason)

Tip! Be careful with your spelling, particularly with words like *because* and *although*.

4 Join the sentences about Martin and his friend John with *which* or *who*.

Example Last Saturday I went to town with John. He wanted to buy a CD.

Last Saturday I went to town with John, who wanted to buy a CD.

1 We cycled into town together. It was fun.
2 However, we couldn't find a music shop. That was annoying.
3 We asked a boy in the street. He told us about a good music shop.
4 However, the shop was closed. It was a pity.
5 We cycled all the way home again. It made us really tired.

> **Remember!**
> You can add extra information to sentences using the words **which** or **who**, e.g. *I've got a friend called John. He loves music.* – *I've got a friend called John, **who** loves music.*
> *John's parents gave him some money for his birthday. It made him really happy.* – *John's parents gave him some money for his birthday, **which** made him really happy.*

Grammar Tenses

5 Match the sentences with the correct tense.

1 I <u>didn't take</u> my umbrella because it was a fine day.   a past continuous
2 I <u>was walking</u> to the swimming pool when it started to rain.   b past perfect
   c past simple
3 I was really sorry I'd <u>forgotten</u> my umbrella.

> **Tip!** Try to use a variety of structures in your writing where you can. This is especially important if you are writing a story.

6 🎧 04 Complete the short story about Kara with a suitable tense. Then listen and check your answers.

Kara and her dad were at home one evening. Kara's dad (0) ..was cooking.. (cook) and Kara (1) .... (watch) TV. Suddenly she (2) .... (hear) someone at the door, so she (3) .... (go) downstairs. Her grandmother (4) .... (come) to visit, and was in the kitchen with her dad. Then Kara (5) .... (see) a small parcel which (6) .... (lie) on the kitchen table – with Kara's name on it! Her grandmother (7) .... (bring) it for her! She (8) .... (open) the parcel. Inside was the most beautiful ring she (9) .... (ever see). Her grandmother (10) .... (buy) it for Kara's birthday.

Grammar Adverbs

👁 PET candidates often make mistakes with the spelling of adverbs.

7 Complete the end of the story about Kara with an adverb from the box.

| fortunately   perfectly   carefully   happily   anxiously kindly |

> **Tip!** Putting adverbs into your story can help to make it more interesting to read.

'I hope the ring fits you, Kara,' said her grandmother (1) ....
Kara (2) .... took the ring out of the box, and put it on her finger.
(3) .... it fitted her (4) .... – it was just the right size! 'It's wonderful, Grandma!' cried Kara (5) .... 'It's the best present I've ever had!' 'You deserve it, Kara,' said her grandmother (6) .... 'You've worked really hard this year. Happy birthday!'

Test 1 Exam practice — Writing • Part 3

Write an answer to **one** of the questions (**7** or **8**) in this part.
Write your answer in about **100 words** on your answer sheet.

Tip! You must begin the letter correctly (*Dear Kate, Hi Sam*) and end it properly too (*Best wishes, Love from*). You could also use *I'm looking forward to hearing from you / seeing you.*

Question 7

- This is part of a letter you receive from an English friend.

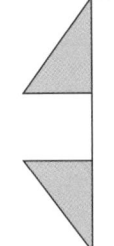

> I'm coming to visit your town in the summer with my parents and my twin brother. My parents love old buildings, and my brother and I just want something fun to do! Can you give me some ideas about where we could go?

- Now write a letter to your friend.
- Write your **letter** on your answer sheet.

Advice

7 You are writing to your friend to give some ideas. Who are the ideas for? Make sure you include all the people. What kind of old buildings are there near where you live? What about activities that your friend and his twin brother will enjoy?

8 Your story must follow on from the sentence. Think about how you can develop your story from the sentence. Where did Tom's dad pick him up? What was inside the bag from the sports shop? Why did Tom's dad smile? What did Tom do next?

Question 8

- Your English teacher has asked you to write a story.
- Your story must begin with this sentence:

   When Tom's dad picked him up in the car, he handed Tom a big bag from a sports store, and smiled.

- Write your **story** on your answer sheet.

Tip! It's important to give your story a definite ending if you can. Don't just stop writing when you think you've done about 100 words.

Test 1 Training Listening Part 1

In this part you:
- **listen**   to one or two people talking in seven short situations
- **match**   what they say with a picture

Vocabulary People

1 What do the boy and girl look like? Describe these features.

age   hair   eyes   face shape   expression   clothes

> **Remember!**
> Nouns to describe people can be countable or uncountable:
> *She's got long **hair**. He's got a small **nose**.*
> Some nouns are usually used in the plural:
> *She's got big **eyes**. He's got dark **eyebrows**.*

2 Look at pictures A–C below and make notes on what each girl looks like.

      A   B   C

3 **05** Listen to a girl called Cassie talking to her friend. Which picture above shows Cassie's sister, A, B or C?

> **Tip!** Read and listen to the focus question carefully.

4 Look at three pictures of a boy. What's happening in each one? Why might the boy be doing these activities?

      A   B   C

5 **06** Listen to a conversation about the boy. How does he plan to train for his big race?

Vocabulary Descriptions

6 Describe the houses to a partner. What makes each house different?

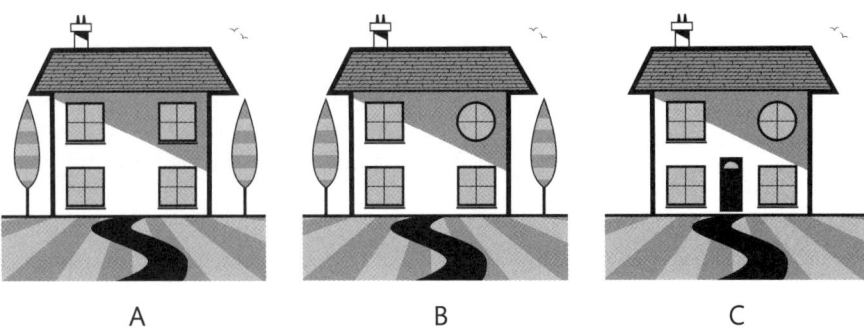

A   B   C

7 🎧 07 Listen to a boy called Jamie talking about where he lives. Which picture above shows his house?

8 Describe one of the T-shirts below to a partner.

A   B   C

9 🎧 08 Listen to a girl called Samantha talking about her T-shirts. Which T-shirt above does she decide to wear to the party?

Tip! Keep a notebook to record all the new words you learn.

10 Look at three pictures of lunchboxes. What's in each one?

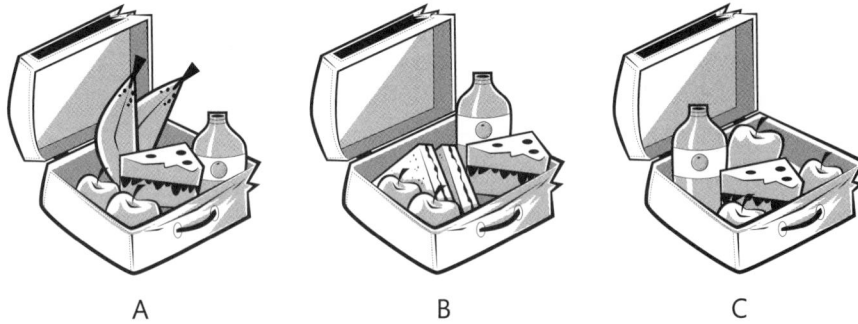

A   B   C

11 🎧 09 Listen to a girl telling her friend what's in her school lunchbox for today. Which picture above shows the girl's lunchbox?

Listening Part 1   Test 1 Training | 35

Test 1 Exam practice — Listening • Part 1

Questions 1 – 7

There are seven questions in this part.
For each question, choose the correct answer (**A**, **B** or **C**).

Tip! Listen carefully to each recording. The key information you need to answer the question may come anywhere – not always at the beginning.

Example: What will the boy have for dinner?

A   (B)   C

1   Which concert did they go to?

A   B   C

2   Which photo will the boy send in to the competition?

  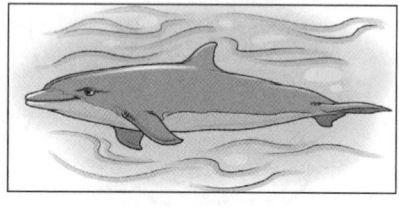

A   B   C

Advice

1 Was it raining at the concert? Was there a light show? Were there big screens?

2 The boy agrees that the picture the girl saw first is the best one for the competition. Which picture was it?

3 Which way will the boy cycle home?

A    B    C

4 What does the boy's new football shirt look like?

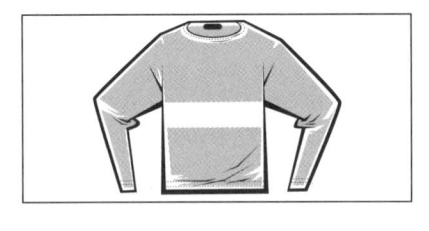

A 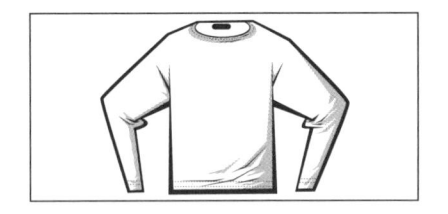   B 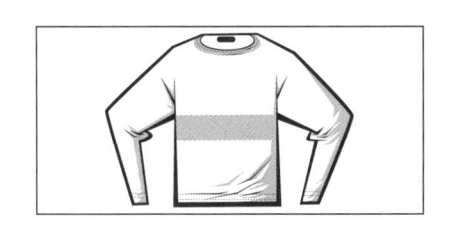   C

5 Where did the boy's teacher put his drawing?

A    B 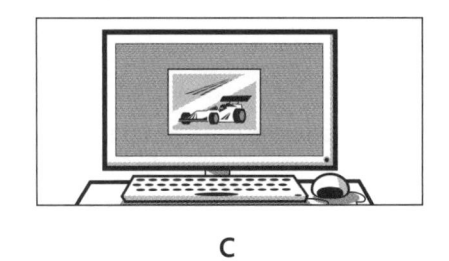   C

6 Where did the friends arrange to meet?

A 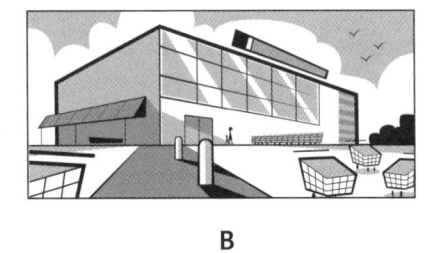   B    C

7 What will the girl take on the school trip?

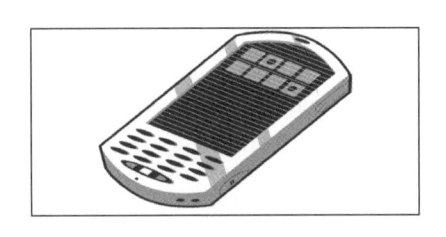

A    B    C

Test 1 Training Listening Part 2

In this part you:
- **listen** to one or two speakers talking about a topic
- **answer** six multiple-choice questions

Vocabulary Time expressions

1 Complete the sentences with an appropriate time expression.

1 I fell off my bike .... I was riding past the school. Luckily I wasn't hurt!
2 .... my teacher explained the Maths question that I understood it.
3 .... I'd finished my shopping, I went home.
4 Yesterday I made a cake. .... I measured the ingredients and then I mixed them well.
5 I woke up to find it had snowed heavily .... the night!
6 .... I'd left my house and cycled off, I realised my bag was still in my room!

Tip! You may need to understand when things happen to answer the questions in Part 2.

Remember! You may hear speakers use some of the following time words and expressions:
before, when, then, while, after, it wasn't until, finally, during, immediately, first of all, whenever, as soon as

Focus Multiple-choice questions

2 🎧 11 Listen to a young guitarist called Jon talking about when he started playing the guitar. When did Jon begin to play the guitar?

1 when he was a young child
2 while he was at secondary school
3 after he'd started college

Tip! If you're not sure of the answer the first time you listen, try to cross out any options you think are definitely wrong. Confirm the correct answer when you listen the second time.

3 Listen again. Cross out the wrong time word or phrase in each sentence.

Example Jon had always been keen on music, even **after** / **before** he started school.

1 Jon used to dance around the room *as soon as / whenever* music was playing.
2 *As soon as / Before* Jon started school, he had some music lessons.
3 Jon played the piano *first of all / immediately*.
4 *Later / Finally* Jon met a good music teacher.
5 Jon knew *immediately / first of all* that the guitar was the right instrument for him.
6 *It was when / It wasn't until* Jon got to college that he realised how much he'd learned.

4 🎧 12 Listen to a girl called Holly talking about joining her school football team. Why did she enjoy her extra practice for the team?

1 The atmosphere was better than her usual classes.
2 She liked attending early in the morning.
3 A lot of her friends went too.

Remember! In Part 2 you may hear speakers explaining and giving reasons for things:
because, in order to, but, since, if, so that, so, although, as, unless

Test 1 Exam practice — Listening • Part 2

Questions 8 – 13

You will hear an interview with a teenager called Amy Manero, who is talking about her interest in music, particularly jazz piano. For each question, choose the correct answer **A**, **B** or **C**.

Tip! The questions come in order of the text. Read each one carefully before you listen so that you don't lose your place while you're listening.

8   When did Amy have lessons with a piano teacher?
   A   at the age of four
   B   before she started secondary school
   C   after getting advice from her school music teacher

9   How did Amy feel at her first big public event?
   A   excited because she was wearing a wonderful costume
   B   nervous because it was her first time on stage
   C   surprised because the audience was very big

10   What does Amy say about playing jazz with the school band?
   A   She was better at it than the rest of the players.
   B   She put lots of effort into learning about it.
   C   She enjoyed it as soon as she started.

11   Amy gives piano lessons so that she can
   A   help people who couldn't normally afford them.
   B   encourage lots of young people to play the piano.
   C   improve her own playing technique.

12   Why does Amy write a blog on the internet?
   A   to get some experience for becoming a journalist
   B   to tell people about her daily life as a musician
   C   to recommend events for people to go to

13   Why does Amy love music so much?
   A   People can understand it whatever their language.
   B   She meets people she likes through playing it.
   C   It brings together people of different ages.

Advice

8 When did Amy start having piano lessons? When did she give up?

*9 Did Amy know a lot of people would come and watch her? Why does she say **I had no idea ...**?*

Test 1 Training — Listening Part 3

In this part you:
- **listen** to one person talking about a topic
- **complete** some notes

Vocabulary Transport

1. Name the unusual means of transport below. If you could choose any means of transport you wished, which one would you choose?

Focus Completing notes

2. Imagine you are about to set off with a group on a journey along a road through the jungle. Look at your notes below. What words might fit in the spaces?

Tip! Before you start listening in Part 3, read through the notes and think what kind of word is missing.

MY JUNGLE JOURNEY NOTES

	Your answers	Sarah's answers
We're going to leave our camp at	1 .... a.m.	1 .... a.m.
We'll travel by	2	2 ....
We'll take plenty of	3	3 ....
The weather will probably be	4	4 ....
On the way, we might see	5	5 ....
We'll stop to rest near a	6	6 ....

Remember! In this part of the test, you have to add words to a set of notes while you are listening to someone talking. Most spaces are single words, numbers or short noun phrases.

3. **CD 1 14** Listen to a woman called Sarah who is going on a trip through the jungle. Fill in her information in the notes above.

Tip! You will hear different numbers or times that might fit the space, but only one of them will be correct.

Test 1 Exam practice — Listening • Part 3

Questions 14 – 19

You will hear a boy called Adam telling his class about a hot air balloon flight he went on.
For each question, fill in the missing information in the numbered space.

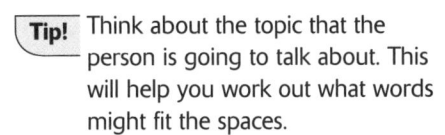

Tip! Think about the topic that the person is going to talk about. This will help you work out what words might fit the spaces.

ADAM'S HOT AIR BALLOON FLIGHT

The flight in the balloon lasted for **(14)** ....

Adam could see as far as the **(15)** .... from the balloon.

Adam didn't recognise a local **(16)** .... from the air.

Adam was surprised that it was **(17)** .... in the balloon basket.

Adam didn't like having to **(18)** .... in the basket.

The balloon finally landed on a **(19)** ....

Advice

14 What kind of word are you looking for? How long would a flight last, do you think?

15 What does Adam say? 'I could see all the way ...'

Test 1 Training — Listening Part 4

In this part you:
- **listen** to an informal conversation between two people
- **understand** the attitudes and opinions of the two people, and the facts they mention

Vocabulary Films

1 Discuss these questions in pairs.
  1 What kind of films do you enjoy watching?
  2 Do you watch them at home or at the cinema?

2 Match the words below with the types of film.

| comedies | documentaries | action and adventure films |
| cartoons | horror films | |

  1 frightening   4 sad   7 clever
  2 exciting   5 funny   8 interesting
  3 scary   6 amazing   9 educational

Vocabulary Attitude and opinion

3 You are going to hear a boy called Max and a girl called Alice talking about films. Before you listen, look carefully at the sentences below. Underline the words that show attitude and opinion.

  1 Max wanted Alice to watch a certain film on TV last night.
  2 Alice usually enjoys watching the films that Max recommends to her.
  3 Alice agrees with Max that the film he mentioned was disappointing.

> **Tip!** Key words in the six sentences will tell you what opinion or attitude to listen for.

> **Remember!**
> Verbs and adjectives can show attitude and opinion.
> surprised, bored, sure, disappointed, certain, confident, keen, annoyed, grateful, worried
> believe, agree, disagree, accept, doubt, think, enjoy, want

4 🎧 16 Listen to Max and Alice talking. Are sentences 1–3 correct or incorrect?

> **Tip!** There is sometimes a question about whether the speakers agree with each other or not. Question 3 is an example of this.

5 🎧 17 Listen to the rest of the conversation. If the sentence is correct, choose A for YES. If it is not correct, choose B for NO.

		YES	NO
1	Max is confident they can find a DVD that Alice will enjoy.	A	B
2	Alice is keen to go to the DVD store with Max.	A	B
3	Max is worried that the DVD store might already be closed.	A	B

Vocabulary Key words

6 These are examples of key words that you might see in Part 4 sentences. Match them with what each speaker says.

1 suggest   Peter: 'That film wasn't as good as everyone said – what a pity!'
2 doubt   Jane: 'Thanks for the invitation to the cinema – I'll come!'
3 accept   Louis: 'Oh, please watch the film with me, Ben! It'll be great!'
4 try to persuade   Mari: 'I know everyone in my class will love this film!'
5 disappointed   Benjamin: 'I'm not sure I'll enjoy that film – I don't really like cartoons.'
6 surprised   Jo: 'Why don't we ask our mum to book our tickets online?'
7 confident   Kasia: 'That cinema is *really* nice inside! I didn't expect that!'

Test 1 Exam practice — Listening • Part 4

18 Questions 20 – 25

Look at the six sentences for this part.
You will hear a boy, Jack, and a girl, Mandy, talking about sports programmes on TV.
Decide if each sentence is correct or incorrect.
If it is correct, choose the letter **A** for **YES**. If it is not correct, choose the letter **B** for **NO**.

Tip! Make sure you listen for the opinion of the correct speaker in each question – some questions ask you for the opinion of *both* speakers.

		YES	NO
20	Mandy knows that Jack is a fan of sports programmes on TV.	A	B
21	Mandy accepts Jack's invitation to watch a sports programme at his house.	A	B
22	Jack agrees with Mandy that there's currently too much sport on TV.	A	B
23	Jack thinks TV sports programmes encourage young people to take up sport.	A	B
24	Mandy suggests that Jack should take part in more sports activities.	A	B
25	Jack persuades Mandy to watch him perform in a sporting event soon.	A	B

Advice

20 Why is Mandy surprised to see Jack in town? Why does she say 'I thought you'd be ...'?

21 What is Mandy hoping to do tonight? So is she going to Jack's house?

Test 1 Training   Speaking Part 1

In this part you:
- **talk**   to an interlocutor for 2–3 minutes
- **answer**   some general questions about yourself

1 The photo shows two people taking their Speaking Test. Match each person with what they do.

1	a **candidate**	a	takes the exam with you
2	the **interlocutor**	b	decides on the marks you get
3	the **assessor**	c	takes the exam
4	the **candidate's partner**	d	asks the questions

Tip! Learn the words you'll need to talk about yourself, your studies and the things you like doing.

Focus Personal questions

2 Write answers for the questions.
1. What is your surname?   ....
2. How do you spell that?   ....
3. Where do you live?   ....
4. Do you study English at school?   ....

3 Match the questions from phase 2 of Part 1 with the candidate's answers.

1. Do you like English?
2. Why do you like English?
3. What's your favourite school subject?
4. Why do you like it?
5. Tell us about your English teacher.
6. What do you enjoy doing in your free time?
7. Tell us about your family.

a. Because I enjoy working with numbers and it's useful in my daily life.
b. I really like maths, although my friends don't!
c. Well, skateboarding and shopping are my favourite activities.
d. Yes, I do. I have lessons every Wednesday.
e. Because it's really useful for writing to my penfriend!
f. I've got two older brothers and a younger sister – she looks a lot like me!
g. She's really nice. She teaches us lots of grammar, but she always makes it fun.

Tip! In phase 2 you can be asked about present and past experiences and future plans.

Focus Listening

4 🔊 19 Listen and complete the interlocutor's questions
1. .... you enjoy .... English?
2. .... us about your ....
3. What did you do ....?
4. .... do you .... doing in your ....?
5. .... you think English will be .... to you in the ....?

Tip! It is important to listen carefully to the interlocutor's questions.

Test 1 Exam practice — Speaking • Part 1

(2–3 minutes)

Phase 1
Interlocutor

> **Tip!** Listen carefully to the interlocutor's questions, and ask if you haven't understood anything.

A/B Good morning / afternoon / evening.
Can I have your marksheets, please?
(Hand over the marksheets to the Assessor)

A/B I'm .... (name) and this is my colleague .... (name).
He / she is just going to listen to us.

A Now, what's your name?
Thank you.

B And what's your name?
Thank you.

B Candidate B, what's your surname?
How do you spell it?
Thank you.

A And, Candidate A, what's your surname?
How do you spell it?
Thank you.

A/B Where do you live / come from?
Do you study English at school?
Do you like it?
Thank you.

Do you live in ...?
Do you have English lessons?

Phase 2
Interlocutor

(The interlocutor may ask one or more of the following questions.)

What's your favourite sport? Why?

How will English be useful to you in the future?

What do you like doing after school?

Tell us about the area where you live.

Thank you.

Advice

Phase 1 *Which is your **surname**? Practise spelling it.*

Phase 2 *If you **don't** enjoy sport, what can you say?*

Test 1 Training Speaking Part 2

In this part you:
- **look at** some information that the interlocutor will give you
- **discuss** your views and opinions with your partner

Focus Suggesting, agreeing and disagreeing

1. 🎧 20 Look at the four places your teachers have suggested for a school trip. Listen to Max and Sophie talking about the four places. Where does Max want to go? Why? What about Sophie? What do they finally agree?

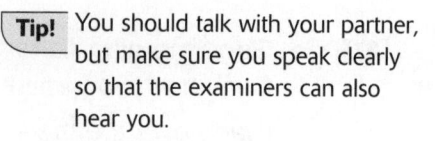

   a)   b)   c)   d)

   > **Tip!** You should talk with your partner, but make sure you speak clearly so that the examiners can also hear you.

   > **Remember!**
   > Here are some phrases to use in Part 2.
   > I think we should ... I don't think we should ... I'm not sure about ...
   > Why don't we ...? Yes, why don't we do that? That's a great idea!
   > How about ...? That's a good idea, but ...
   > I'm not sure we should ... What do you think?
   > I don't think ..., do you?

2. 🎧 20 Read what Max and Sophie said. Listen again and complete their conversation.

   Max: So which one (1) .... is a good idea for the school trip, Sophie? (2) .... the zoo? A lot of people would really enjoy that – including me!

   Sophie: I'm (3) .... go there. Some people don't like to see wild animals in a zoo. I (4) .... go to the concert instead. The whole class likes listening to music!

   Max: That's (5) .... we all like different kinds of music. And (6) .... anyone will choose the museum, (7) ....? We've been there before.

   Sophie: Mm, so that just leaves the beach. (8) .... go there?

   Max: (9) ....! Everyone will enjoy that!

3. Now talk with your partner about which place you would both choose to go for a school trip.

4. Your youth club has some money to spend. Your youth club leader has asked you all what you'd like to do to make an empty room at the club look more attractive to use. In pairs discuss these ideas.

   > **Tip!** In Part 2, talk about all the ideas in the task, and suggest others if you can.

   paint the room different colours   put things on the walls
   buy new items to put in the room

Test 1 Exam practice — Speaking • Part 2

(2–3 minutes)

Tip! Remember to talk about the things in the pictures – don't just talk generally.

Interlocutor
(to both candidates)

> I'm going to describe a situation to you.
>
> You are going on a **cycling trip** in the countryside with a group of friends. You need to decide **what things would be useful** to put in your **backpack** and **take with you**. Talk together about the **different things** it would be **best** to take.
>
> Here is a picture with some ideas to help you.

*Place **Test 1 Exam practice Speaking Part 2** picture (see page C1) in front of candidates.*

> I'll say that again.
>
> You are going on a **cycling trip** in the countryside with a group of friends. You need to decide **what things would be useful** to put in your **backpack** and **take with you**. Talk together about the **different things** it would be **best** to take.

> All right? Talk together.

Allow the candidates enough time to complete the task without interruption. Prompt only if necessary.

> Thank you. (Can I have the booklet please?)

Advice
Are there any things here that might not be so useful? What about the swimming things? What will the weather be like? Will you need the jacket? Is it safe to wear headphones while you're cycling?

🎧 21 **Listen to two students doing the task above.**

Test 1 Training Speaking Part 3

In this part you:
- **talk** to the interlocutor about a colour photo
- **say** what you can see in the photo

Vocabulary Describing people, things and events

1. Look around your classroom. What can you see? Try to describe the room and some of the people in it as fully as you can!

2. Describe this photo to a partner. Where are the people? What are they doing? What can you say about the people in it?

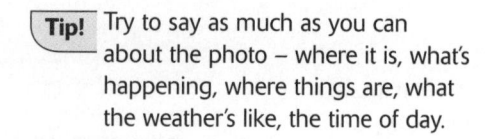

Tip! Try to say as much as you can about the photo – where it is, what's happening, where things are, what the weather's like, the time of day.

Remember!
If you're describing position, you'll need to use some of these expressions:
on the left, on the right, behind, near, next to, between, above, below, in the corner, through, outside, beyond.

You may need words to talk about the weather if you're describing something outside:

It's: sunny, raining, pouring with rain, windy, snowy, freezing cold, foggy, cloudy, warm, hot.

3. 🎧 22 Listen to a student talking about the photo. What does she say about the people in it? Did she mention anything that you missed?

Tip! Think about what tense you need to use if you're describing what people are doing at the moment.

Test 1 Exam practice — Speaking • Part 3

(3 minutes)

Interlocutor
(to both candidates)

> Now I'd like both of you to talk on your own about something. I'm going to give both of you a photograph of **children meeting with their friends**.
>
> Candidate A, here is your photograph. Please show it to Candidate B, but I'd like you to talk about it.
>
> *(Place **Test 1 Exam practice Speaking Part 3** picture (see page C7) in front of Candidate A.)*
>
> Candidate B, you just listen. I'll give you your photograph in a moment.

(Candidate A)

(Approximately 1 minute)

If there is a need to intervene, prompts rather than direct questions should be used.

Interlocutor

> Thank you.

> Now, Candidate B, here is your photograph. It also shows **teenagers meeting with their friends**. Please show it to Candidate A, and tell us what you can see in the photograph.
>
> *(Place **Test 1 Exam practice Speaking Part 3** picture (see page C8) in front of Candidate B.)*

(Candidate B)

(Approximately 1 minute)

> Thank you.

🎧 23 Listen to a student talking about Photo A.

🎧 24 Listen to a student talking about Photo B.

Test 1 Training — Speaking Part 4

In this part you:
- talk with your partner
- talk about the same topic as in Part 3

Focus Talking with a partner

1 🎧 **25** Listen and complete what Maggie and Ralph say about picnics and where they like to eat.

Ralph
Well, **(1)** .... my family and what we eat.
My father cooks great steaks **(2)** .... he loves meat.
I think he's really **(3)** .... making desserts, too. His cheesecake is the **(4)** ....!
How **(5)** ....? **(6)** .... often go for picnics?

Maggie
We **(7)** .... at home.
We always have lots of different dishes **(8)** .... my father's American and my mother's Italian. She makes pasta with **(9)** .... sauces, and also **(10)** .... salads. I **(11)** .... the food they cook, and my parents really **(12)** .... doing it **(13)** .... it's a change from work.
(14) .... to a restaurant with your family?

> **Tip!** Don't forget to look at your partner while you're talking together.

> **Remember!**
> Phrases for asking for your partner's opinion, giving your opinion, and giving reasons for your opinion:
> I think, I don't think, I prefer ... because, I love, I enjoy it so I, ...
> What do you think? How about you?
> Do you like ...?

2 🎧 **26** Listen and complete the second part of the conversation with phrases for agreeing and disagreeing.

Maggie:	It's great to go out for a meal with your family or friends.
Ralph:	Mm, **(1)** .... We often eat out with our relatives.
Maggie:	So have you ever been to a restaurant with your family?
Ralph:	Yes, lots of times and I love pizza restaurants!
Maggie:	**(2)** ....!
Ralph:	But I don't like burger bars or cafés much.
Maggie:	**(3)** .... Anyway, there aren't many cafés where we live, are there?
Ralph:	**(4)** .... there's a good one in the town centre. That serves great milk shakes – oh, and cake and ice cream and things.
Maggie:	Really? I must go there sometime. I love ice cream!
Ralph:	**(5)** ....? ....!

> **Remember!**
> Phrases for responding to, agreeing or disagreeing:
> I agree. I don't agree. I'm not sure.
> So do I. Neither do I. Me too.
> Yes, but ..., No, but ..., Do you? I don't.
> Really? That's amazing / wonderful / exciting / awful / terrible!

3 In pairs, take turns to read out sentences 1–6. Your partner must respond by agreeing, disagreeing or making a comment of some kind. Then if you can, ask another question to keep the conversation going.

A — I love coffee. Do you? I don't! — B

A — I like getting presents. So do I! — B

A — It's minus 20 in my country right now. Really? That's amazing! — B

1 I enjoy shopping.
2 I want to travel to the moon!
3 I don't like cold weather.
4 I've got 14 cousins.
5 I prefer watching DVDs to going to the cinema.
6 My great-grandmother is 101 years old.

Test 1 Exam practice — Speaking • Part 4

(3 minutes)

Tip! Don't worry too much about making a grammar mistake – just keep talking together with your partner.

Interlocutor
(to both candidates)

> Your photographs showed **children and teenagers meeting their friends**. Now I'd like you to talk together about the kind of things you do when **you** meet your friends when you're **not** at school and say **why** you like doing these things together.

Allow the students enough time to complete the task without intervention. Prompt only if necessary.

> Thank you. That's the end of the test.

🎧 27 Listen to some additional questions on this topic and give your answers.

Advice

1 Think about all the different things you might do with your friends: Play sports? Go to the cinema? Meet at friends' houses? Go to the park? Go swimming? Go to parties? How could you develop these answers? Be prepared to give more detail.

2 Don't forget to invite your partner to join in the conversation too. Look at him / her and don't do all the talking yourself.

Test 2 Training — Reading Part 1

- What kind of texts do you have to read in Part 1?
- What are you looking for when you choose your answer A, B or C?

Vocabulary Formal and informal language

1 Look at this sign and answer the questions.

> IT IS STRICTLY FORBIDDEN TO WALK ON THE GRASS

1 What does *forbidden* mean?
2 Are you allowed to walk on the grass?

Check your answer with a partner. Where might you see a sign like this?

Tip! It's important to look for words and expressions that have similar meanings.

2 Look at the formal verbs 1–9 below. They often appear in signs and notices. Match them with the meanings in the box.

| take away | don't allow | put off | call off | allow | pick up |
| leave | put | ~~tell~~ | ask | | |

Example inform ....*tell*....

1 request ....
2 cancel ....
3 forbid ....
4 place ....
5 remove ....
6 depart ....
7 postpone ....
8 collect ....
9 permit ....

Tip! Phrasal verbs are often used in the options A–C, and in informal messages, so learn as many as you can. (See also Test 2 Reading Part 5.)

Remember!

put	+ away	take	+ back
	+ on		+ out
	+ down		+ up
	+ up		+ away
	+ off		

3 Look at the verbs in the Remember box. In pairs, check that you know what they mean. Can you use each one in a sentence?

4 Complete the sentences with a formal verb from exercise 2.

Example Passengers are ..*informed*.. that mobile phone use is strictly forbidden.

1 Any bicycles left outside this shop will be ....
2 Buses .... from this stop every 20 minutes.
3 Students are not .... to borrow more than six books at a time.
4 Due to bad weather, today's football match is .... until next week.
5 Homework should be .... from Mr Brown before 4 p.m. today.
6 Pupils are .... not to use computers without a teacher present.

5 What signs do *you* see around your school? What do they mean in English? Make a list with a partner.

Vocabulary Modal verbs

6a Circle the correct modal verb in each sentence.

1. In a lot of schools, you *should / must / can* wear a uniform. You can't wear anything else.
2. If I were you, I *could / will / would* go to the Youth Centre if you want to make friends.
3. You *mustn't / won't / shan't* be late for classes. It's against the rules.
4. You *need to / can / might* bring your own lunch – it's OK to do that if you don't like the canteen food.

> **Tip!** You may need to understand the meanings of different modal verbs to understand Part 1 texts and options.

> **Remember!**
> can / can't   shall / shan't   might
> ought to   must /mustn't   may
> would / wouldn't   will/ won't   could
> need to   should / shouldn't

b Which sentence above:
a. gives advice?
b. says that something is definitely **not** allowed?
c. says that something has to be done?
d. says that something **is** allowed?

👁 PET candidates often make mistakes with modal verbs.

7 Cross out and correct the mistake in each sentence.

Example   If you ~~would go~~ on holiday with your friends, you would have more fun.   ....**went**....

1. I'm really sorry but I **need to missing** your class today.   ....
2. I **must to tell** you what happened to me recently.   ....
3. A friend of mine and I **shall go** to the cinema this evening.   ....
4. I think you **should chose** the holiday with your friend.   ....
5. You **must going** to the cinema at 4.30 p.m.   ....
6. I **would to buy** a film.   ....
7. If you like action movies, I think we **shall see** *Killer Max*.   ....
8. I **need tell** you about my holiday in Piura.   ....

Focus Who's talking to whom?

8 Look at the text message and answer the questions.

1. Who is the message to?   ....
2. Who needs to be picked up?   ....
3. Who is it from?   ....
4. Who can't pick them up?   ....
5. Who's going to drive the car?   ....

> Hi Maria! My mum has to work late tonight, so my sister Jane's coming instead to take us home in her car at 6. Hope that's OK. See you later. Fran

> **Tip!** It's important in the informal texts – notes, texts messages, emails – to decide who's talking to whom.

Reading Part 1

Test 2 Exam practice — Reading • Part 1

Questions 1 – 5

Look at the text in each question.
What does it say?
Mark the correct letter **A**, **B** or **C** on your answer sheet.

> **Tip!** Take the time to read the three options A, B and C carefully – they may sometimes look close in meaning, but only <u>one</u> will be completely correct.

Example:

0

> Hi Jon. Your friend Mark came to the house earlier to see if you were in. Can you ring him back before 5.30 tonight? He's going to football practice then.
> Mum

Mum is texting Jon to

A tell him to contact his friend.

B remind him that it's football practice tonight.

C ask if he'll be home before 5.30.

Answer: 0 **A** B C

1

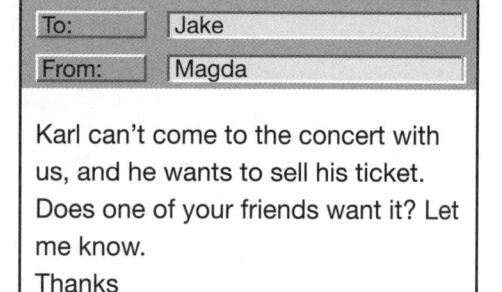

> To: Jake
> From: Magda
>
> Karl can't come to the concert with us, and he wants to sell his ticket. Does one of your friends want it? Let me know.
> Thanks

A Karl wants Jake to buy him an extra ticket for the concert.

B Jake has told Magda that there's now a spare concert ticket available.

C Magda wonders whether Jake knows anyone keen to buy Karl's concert ticket.

2

> You are requested not to leave bicycles outside these gates during school hours.

A It is forbidden to leave bikes here at any time of day.

B You may not leave your bike here except when the school is closed.

C Bikes should be left inside these gates after school hours.

Advice

1 Look at <u>who</u> is writing the email to <u>whom</u>.

2 When <u>can</u> you leave your bicycle outside the gates?

3

> Students are reminded that mobiles are forbidden in classrooms – place them in lockers provided.

A Students must leave phones in the correct place instead of keeping them during lessons.

B Students are not allowed to bring their phones into school at all.

C Students can use their phones in classrooms if they lock them away afterwards.

4

> Hi Sam,
> I'm waiting for you here at the swimming pool with Jamie – where are you? Did you forget? Or is your bus late again? Hurry up!
> Alex

A Sam is expecting to turn up late to meet his friends at the pool.

B Alex is impatient for Sam to join him and Jamie at the pool.

C Sam's friends are worried that he's changed his mind about going to the pool.

5

> To: All students
> From: Mrs Draper, dance teacher
>
> Well done, everyone, for the dance performance for parents last night. You did everything right! Only two more performances to go and then you can relax!

Mrs Draper is emailing to

A inform all students when the last dance performance will be.

B suggest ways of improving the dance performance.

C encourage students to keep up their good work.

Advice

3 What should students do with their mobiles during lessons?

4 Who is the text message from? How is he feeling? Why?

5 Is Mrs Draper happy with the students' dancing?

Test 2 Training — Reading Part 2

- How many short texts do you have to read in Part 2?
- What do you have to do with the descriptions of people?

1 This training section includes a text about days out. Where do you like to go on a day out with family or friends? Why? Look at the list below and talk with a partner.

> the beach   the cinema   shopping   a sports event   the zoo
> sightseeing in a city   a museum or gallery   the countryside

Focus Paraphrasing

2 Look at the words and expressions below. You might see them in texts about days out. Match 1–10 with the meanings a–j.

1 open at the weekends
2 by the sea
3 vehicles
4 public transport
5 suitable for teenagers
6 cheap, cheaper, not too expensive
7 somewhere to have a meal
8 crowded
9 away from the crowds
10 go to the cinema

a great for young people aged 13–19
b watch a movie, see a film
c a restaurant, a café
d busy, too many people
e a reasonable price, a discount, reduced
f quiet, peaceful, not very busy
g on the coast, near the beach
h cars, vans, lorries
i 9–6 p.m. daily, including Saturday and Sunday
j train, bus

Tip! To find the answers in Part 2 you might need to paraphrase (read and understand the same thing written in a different way), using different words or phrases.

Focus Skimming and scanning

3 Read this text quickly, then do the task below.

> The Film Museum in Castle Street was built in 1975, and opened four years later. It displays costumes and items for creating special effects that date from when moving pictures first began.
> Last year it was visited by the actor Tom Drake, and there are regular visits and talks with well-known film stars. The Museum is open every day apart from Sunday, and entry costs £4.75.

Tip! When you start Part 2 you need to read through the texts as quickly as you can to get the main idea (*skim*), before you read for details (*scan*). See how much information you can remember!

What can you remember about the text? Try these steps.

a Write down any words or ideas you can remember.
b Share what you've written with a partner.
c Answer questions your teacher will ask you about the text.

Test 2 Exam practice — Reading • Part 2

Questions 6 – 10

The people below are all looking for a park to visit that has lots of different attractions.
On the next page there are reviews of eight parks.
Decide which park would be the most suitable for the following people to go to.
For questions **6–10**, mark the correct letter **(A–H)** on your answer sheet.

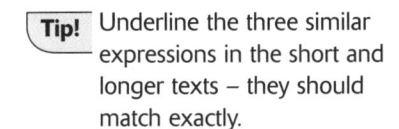

Tip! Underline the three similar expressions in the short and longer texts – they should match exactly.

---

6 Fran and her family love rides involving water. They want somewhere that offers family tickets with reductions for a two-day visit. As they're coming by public transport, they want a park near a railway station.

7 Rick wants a park by the sea, so that he can swim afterwards. He'd like somewhere that doesn't have big queues for rides, and where he can try driving model vehicles.

8 Maria likes going on big rides where she can have her photo taken during the ride. She also loves cycling in places away from traffic.

9 Jaime likes watching talent shows and also going to animal parks. His family want to find somewhere where they can all eat a good meal together at lunchtime.

10 Sophia loves watching science fiction films. She'd also like somewhere with other indoor attractions in case of bad weather. She loves buying presents for her friends.

Advice

6 There are four texts that mention water. Look carefully at these.

7 Two texts mention the sea – which words are connected with the sea? (e.g. **coast**, **beach**)

8 What other words are connected with cycling? Two texts mention these.

9 Four texts mention animal parks – can you find them? Which one also mentions talent shows and good lunches?

10 Which parks show films?

Reading Part 2 | Test 2 Exam practice | 57

Holiday Parks

A Castle Towers

For cycling fans this is the perfect place – follow the track right through the animal park, past the enormous train ride and back to the free swings and slides. There are also opportunities to perform in the daily talent shows – you could end up a TV star! The railway station is a short walk from the park.

B Ranthorpe

There's plenty to do outdoors here in the animal park. There's also the biggest cinema in the area, with a great collection of movies about space travel in the future, a huge skating rink and an indoor driving track for model cars – have your photo taken driving one! The shops have fantastic souvenirs, and the restaurants serve delicious food.

C Minton Park

Try the Splash Ride on the lake here – perfect for people who enjoy getting wet! If you're with brothers and sisters, get a special discount – you can visit the park again the following day for free! The park is in a very convenient location for people arriving by train.

D Dansmere

Visit the movie theatre and special effects display here if you're keen on science fiction films. The park is huge, so adults can also drive their cars round past the fields of animals and park near the roundabouts. There's a model train to transport people without cars around the park.

E Wickton Manor

This small park is the best place for avoiding crowds. Located on the coast, it's perfect for water sports. The big attractions are the cinema and the car races – whatever your age, have a go in the special small cars around the outdoor track. Wickton is some distance from the station, so it's better to come by car.

F Flamberton

Huge rides are the speciality here – try the fast train or the enormous water slide! And there are cameras along the way to take your picture! Then take a bike and ride along the leafy paths that go around the park – no cars allowed! One-day single and family tickets are available.

G Pensmere

The park is right on the beach and offers fantastic water sports, including high-speed rides in boats across the waves. The restaurants are famous for the quality of their food. However, the park does get busy, so you'll need patience when waiting for rides. Visitors coming by rail will need to take a long taxi ride from the station.

H Parkers Island

If you like watching ordinary people singing and dancing, you'll love the daily performances in the small theatre here. There's also a zoo with rabbits, birds and deer which you can help to feed! Also, the souvenir shops are really good here. And when you're hungry, the fantastic restaurants are open all day – and there are no queues anywhere!

Test 2 Training — Reading Part 3

- What kind of text do you read in Part 3?
- How many questions will you have to answer?

1 This training section includes a text about water and watersports. Look at the pictures below and answer the questions.

1. What sport can you see in each picture?
2. How many words can you think of connected with water?
3. If you had the chance to try a new watersport, which one would you choose? Which ones wouldn't you try? Why not?

Grammar Conditionals – *if* sentences

PET candidates often make mistakes with conditional sentences.

2 Find and correct the mistake in each sentence.

Example I'd be excited too if it ~~would be~~ my sister's wedding. **was or were**

1. If you be careful, you'll be safe. ....
2. He asked me what I'll do if I were him. ....
3. If you choose to go with your parents, they would be happy to see you. ....
4. If you will find it, I will give you a prize. ....
5. Would it be all right if I give you extra work? ....

Tip! In Part 3 you may need to understand *if* sentences about how likely things are to happen.

Remember!
There are three different types of conditional sentence:
a) zero *If you go to the beach early, it's empty.* (talking about something that's always true)
b) 1st *If it rains tomorrow, I won't go to the beach.* (talking about a real possibility)
c) 2nd *If I had enough money, I'd go waterskiing.* (talking about something that's unreal)

3 🎧 28 Complete the text about Marta with the correct form of the verbs in brackets. Then listen and check your answers.

My favourite watersport is windsurfing. I wasn't good at first, but I've discovered that if you **(0)** ...**go**... (go) regularly, you can improve quite quickly. If I **(1)** .... (have) the opportunity, I'd probably try sailing. My dad can't sail, but he's promised that if he has time during the summer, he **(2)** .... (take) me scuba diving. How cool is that? The problem is the weather, though. If it's bad, we probably **(3)** .... (not go). I wish I lived somewhere with better weather – if I **(4)** .... (do), I'd go in the sea every day! But if it's a cold day where I live, you **(5)** .... (not do) watersports – even if it's sunny, the wind **(6)** .... (be) often freezing!

4 Complete the sentences using *unless*.

1. You can't be good at a sport if you don't practise.
   You can't be good at a sport ....
2. You shouldn't go windsurfing if you can't swim.
   You shouldn't go windsurfing ....

Remember!
You can also use *unless* as the negative of *if* in conditional sentences.
I only go swimming if the water's warm.
*I don't go swimming **unless** the water's warm.*

Test 2 Exam practice — Reading • Part 3

Questions 11 – 20

Look at the sentences below about dogs that go surfing in the sea.
Read the text on the opposite page to decide if each sentence is correct or incorrect.
If it is correct, mark **A** on your answer sheet.
If it is not correct, mark **B** on your answer sheet.

> **Tip!** Not all of the information in the text will be needed to answer the questions, so read the questions first and then search for the answer for each one in the text.

11 The article says the current fashion for dogs doing sport started with an internet film.

12 The surfing competition that the article describes was limited to dogs of a certain size.

13 The competition took place on a beach during bad weather.

14 The most important thing in the competition was how long the dogs stayed on the surfboards.

15 Dog owner Jeff had to work hard to encourage his dog Mandy to try surfing.

16 Mandy now knows how to control the direction of the board herself.

17 Mandy has a particular move she makes on the surfboard when she gets to the beach.

18 The owner of Ben the dog is worried that Ben might really dislike the sea.

19 A film-making team who saw Mandy decided she was just what they were looking for.

20 The film that Mandy is in shows the most dangerous surfing moves that the dogs do.

> **Advice**
> **11** Where would you find a 'social networking site'?
> **13** Is 'stormy weather' good or bad?
> **15** Did Mandy like surfing at the beginning? Did she need encouragement to try it?
> **19** What did the 'visiting film crew' think about Mandy?

SURFING DOGS

We've all seen pictures of dogs doing amazing things – but what would you think if you saw one surfing?

Ever since a video of a dog on a skateboard appeared on a social networking site, dogs have become involved in more and more unusual sports. The latest is dog surfing, with dogs taking part in major competitions along with their owners.

In one recent competition, as many as 60 dogs, ranging in size from very big to extremely small, flew in to a seaside resort in the USA and hit the beach, going out on a stormy day to ride the waves on human-sized surfboards. The dogs wore special life jackets so that they'd be safe if they fell in, and were placed on surfboards on shallow waves. They had ten minutes to show what they could do, and were judged not only on the length of their ride but also their confidence and overall ability.

One dog, Mandy, has always loved surfing right from the start. She and her owner Jeff surf together almost every day after Jeff finishes work. 'There's nothing I've trained her to do,' says Jeff. 'She's just a natural. If I pick big waves for her, she just rides them.'

When the pair are in the sea, Jeff holds Mandy's board until the perfect wave arrives and then he lets her go. 'She's learned to make the board go where she wants, and she won't go unless it's a good wave – she'll just wait. Her biggest wave so far has been about 2 metres high, and her longest ride about 100 metres.'

Many dogs hop off the board once they reach shallow water, but Mandy's got style – she always waits till her board's near the beach and then turns herself round on it a couple of times.

One of Mandy's surfing buddies, Ben, is also a star performer. 'There's no way I could make him do it if he didn't want to,' says his owner Julie. 'You just can't stop him. If he falls into the water, we pull him out again, and he just shakes himself then runs back in!'

Mandy has also become a film star. When a visiting film crew saw Mandy perform in a surfing contest, they knew she was exactly right for a role in their new film. Several of the other dogs surfing along with Mandy have also got parts as extras in the film, which with the help of computers shows them surfing really enormous waves – although they'd be in trouble if they tried them in real life!

Test 2 Training — Reading Part 4

- Will there be a long or short text in Part 4?
- What kind of questions will you need to answer?

Vocabulary: Verbs

1 What does each verb in the list mean?

> compare   complain   describe   defend   encourage
> advertise   warn

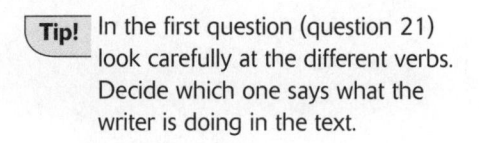

Tip! In the first question (question 21) look carefully at the different verbs. Decide which one says what the writer is doing in the text.

2 These sentences are from a young people's guidebook to a seaside town. What is the writer doing in each sentence? Use the verbs from exercise 1.

Example The beach has wonderful golden sand and the sea is deep blue. — *describing*

1. There's always a lot of traffic in the town centre, so don't try cycling there. ....
2. There are outdoor concerts every weekend at the Royal Gardens during the summer. ....
3. The milkshakes at Bentons café are really awful! ....
4. The beach is much better than any of the others along the coast. ....
5. Lots of people complain about the shops, but actually you can buy good things there. ....
6. You should definitely try the adventure park near the beach – it's cool. ....

👁 PET candidates often make mistakes with verb use and forms.

3 Cross out and correct the verb in these sentences – you may need to use a different verb or change the form or spelling of the verb, or change the word order.

Example We'll see 'Twilight Eclipse', if you don't ~~complain~~. — *mind*

1. We can visit a farm and **warn** about how they take care of the animals. ....
2. My teacher is very friendly and she **encourage** me. ....
3. Now I'll **describe you my bedroom**. ....
4. I'm sorry to **warn** you I'm going to miss your class tomorrow. ....
5. Give me a call and come and see my room, but I **advertise** you it's very untidy. ....
6. I bought a new dress but I don't know how to **explain** it in words. ....

Remember! Here are some more verbs that often appear in Question 21. Make sure you know what they mean: *recommend, advise, inform, offer, persuade*.

Vocabulary Adjectives

4 These adjectives all show attitude and opinion. Match an adjective with each situation below.

> **Tip!** Part 4 asks about the *writer's* attitudes and opinions in a text – not *your* opinions.

| annoyed | shocked | anxious | confused | uncomfortable | grateful |
| hopeful | positive | realistic | curious |

1 Is it this way? Or that way? I really don't know!   ....
2 Thank you so much for helping me!   ....
3 Oh no! There's smoke coming from that building!   ....
4 Hmm – I wonder what that strange object is?   ....
5 Oh dear. I really hope we're not going to be late.   ....
6 Look! My favourite CD's damaged! Now I'll have to buy another one!   ....
7 It'd be nice to win the race, but I just know I haven't practised enough. Oh well, next time!   ....
8 My friend wants me to invite a girl in our class to the party, but I've never even spoken to her before. It'll be a bit embarrassing.   ....
9 It's rained today, but it might be sunny tomorrow, and then we could go to the beach.   ....
10 I got good marks in my last test, so now I'm feeling much better about the next one!   ....

👁 PET candidates often make mistakes with adjectives.

5 These sentences use the adjectives *shocked, annoyed, curious, grateful, confused* and *anxious*. Cross out and correct the adjective in each sentence – you may need to use a different adjective, change the form or spelling of the adjective or use a different preposition.

1 I was very **annoying** because in it I had things I really needed.   ....
2 When I read the email **I'm was confusing** about what was happening.   ....
3 **I have a lot of curious** to know what my town will be like in 20 years' time.   ....
4 I hope the holidays will be **greatfull**.   ....
5 He was very **shocked for** the accident.   ....
6 I'm really **confused** to tell you I'm going to miss your class tomorrow.   ....
7 I opened it, **anxious for reading** the letter from him.   ....
8 I'm so **gratefull with you** for these days with you.   ....

Reading Part 4

Test 2 Exam practice — Reading • Part 4

Questions 21 – 25

Read the text and questions below.
For each question, mark the correct letter **A**, **B**, **C** or **D** on your answer sheet.

Tip! Your answers must come from the text, not from your own knowledge.

Wildlife Art

By Isabelle Ramirez, aged 15

Go Wild! is a touring exhibition of wildlife photos and paintings by young artists. Its last stop has been in my city, and I went last week.

The pictures were produced by teenagers living in countries as far apart as Asia and Canada. There were often humans and animals working together in the pictures, and to me that was the message behind them. In one painting, for example, a girl was resting her head on an elephant. Some wildlife experts say this doesn't show animals as they really are in the wild, and I agree. But that didn't stop the pictures being beautiful. One artist, for example, had filmed videos of animals through coloured glass and another had added music – they worked really well.

There were also action photos. One was of a bear that had climbed up a tree in a garden in Canada and refused to come down. Wildlife experts sent the bear to sleep with a special vet's gun – and a brilliant young photographer saw a great opportunity. He took a photo showing the bear falling out of the tree, fast asleep, onto a rubber mat on the ground, as if it was jumping like a gymnast! The bear was later returned to the wild. And there were lots more amazing pictures like that!

Another young photographer took a photo while swimming with an elephant – although she almost got kicked as a result. I was glad I didn't know that when I first saw the picture! It reminded me that the animals in the pictures were still wild animals, and shouldn't be trusted. But this photographer clearly felt the photo was worth the danger.

21 What is Isabelle Ramirez trying to do in the text?
- **A** say who had done the best pictures in the exhibition
- **B** encourage young people to take up wildlife photography
- **C** give her opinion of different work in the exhibition
- **D** show that wildlife photography isn't as dangerous as it looks

Tip! You may need to read in more than one place in the text to find your answers, particularly in Questions 21 and 25.

22 What does Isabelle think the artists are trying to show?
- **A** that animals and people can live peacefully with each other
- **B** that wild creatures living in nature are very beautiful
- **C** that animals live very differently in different countries
- **D** that films of wildlife are more attractive than photos or paintings

Advice

22 What does Isabelle say was the **message** behind the picture?

23 What does Isabelle say about the person who took the bear photo?

24 Did Isabelle know anything about the elephant picture when she first saw it?

23 What does Isabelle say about the photo of the bear?
- **A** It didn't look very believable.
- **B** It showed one photographer's quick thinking.
- **C** It made her worry about what happened to the bear.
- **D** It was the most unusual photo in the exhibition.

24 When Isabelle saw a girl's photo of an elephant, she
- **A** thought it was worth the girl's swim to get the photo.
- **B** was sure that the girl had disturbed the elephant.
- **C** felt it proved animals don't make good subjects for photos.
- **D** was pleased she only learned the story behind it later.

25 What might people visiting the exhibition in Isabelle's city say about it?

- **A** I'm sure some of these photos aren't real – a girl couldn't really stand so close to an elephant like that!
- **B** These young people have been really lucky to travel so much – it's a pity they didn't take any photos in their own countries.
- **C** I like the way some people have added special effects to their work – really clever!
- **D** I'm glad it's a touring exhibition – that means members of my family can see it when it gets to their city.

Reading Part 4 | Test 2 Exam practice | 65

Test 2 Training Reading Part 5

- What kind of words can you put in the spaces in Part 5?
- How many words do you have to choose from for each space?

Vocabulary Phrasal verbs

1 Circle the correct prepositions to form the phrasal verbs below.

Example set **up** / (**off**) on a journey

1 take *off* / *on* clothes when you want to change
2 take something *away* / *back* to a shop
3 try *out* / *on* new clothes to see if they fit
4 get *up* / *on* first thing in the morning
5 look *around* / *into* a town
6 go *on* / *with* the colours you're wearing
7 look *out* / *after* children
8 get *back* / *off* home after a journey

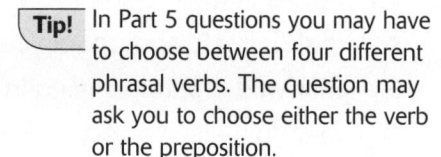

Tip! In Part 5 questions you may have to choose between four different phrasal verbs. The question may ask you to choose either the verb or the preposition.

2 🎧 29 Circle the correct verbs to complete the text about a shopping trip. Then listen and check your answers.

My mum and I had to (0) (*get*) / *go* up at 7 a.m. on Saturday morning so that we could (1) *go* / *set* off early for the town centre. My gran stayed at home and (2) *looked* / *cared* after my baby brother – he hates shopping! When we got to town, we (3) *looked* / *got* around one of the big department stores. I (4) *tried* / *took* on a pair of shoes, but quickly (5) *took* / *put* them off again – they were far too small! Anyway, they didn't (6) *go* / *get* with anything I was wearing. After a bit more shopping, we went home. I was pleased to (7) *take* / *get* back but Mum says she's going again tomorrow to (8) *take* / *return* back a sweater she bought!

Remember! To understand what pronouns mean, you often have to read back in the text. Find the underlined words. Who is *we*? What are *they*?

3 Make sentences using the phrasal verbs in one of these spider diagrams.

```
   off    out         away    in         away    back        down    in
      \  /               \  /               \  /               \  /
      set                give               take              break
      /                  /  \               /  \              /  \
     up                out   up           out   up         into   up
```

Tip! You need to learn as many phrasal verbs as you can.

👁 PET candidates often make mistakes with prepositions.

4 Cross out and correct the preposition in each sentence.

1 I was very excited **for** her answer. ....
2 **In** that moment her mother came home. ....
3 I'd like to thank you **about** your letter. ....
4 Apologise **with** your parents. ....
5 I'm very keen **in** shopping. ....

Test 2 Exam practice — Reading • Part 5

Questions 26 – 35

Read the text below and choose the correct word for each space. For each question, mark the correct letter **A**, **B**, **C** or **D** on your answer sheet.

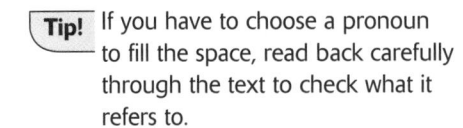

> **Tip!** If you have to choose a pronoun to fill the space, read back carefully through the text to check what it refers to.

Example:

0   **A** taken   **B** made   **C** given   **D** brought

Answer: 0 **A** ▄   B ▢   C ▢   D ▢

Space experiment

Some exciting photos of space have recently appeared on the internet – all **(0)** .... by teenagers!

Using a cheap camera and a simple balloon, some school students got a large **(26)** .... of amazing photos from 15 miles **(27)** .... Earth.

The teacher said, '**(28)** .... carried out an experiment to explore what different **(29)** .... on the Earth look like from space – and prove that you don't have to use expensive equipment as the textbooks say.'

Seventeen-year-old student Miguel reported, 'We'd spent long **(30)** .... working on the experiment after school, but then had to put it **(31)** .... due to the weather. Then we were worried that the balloon **(32)** .... rise higher than 10,000 metres, which wasn't **(33)** .... high enough for our experiment. But in the end it wasn't a problem. And **(34)** .... the balloon had travelled so far, it was still working when it returned! So we've learned that in **(35)** .... life, experiments don't always have to follow the textbooks!'

26	**A**	amount	**B**	sum	**C**	number	**D**	total
27	**A**	among	**B**	above	**C**	about	**D**	along
28	**A**	It	**B**	There	**C**	These	**D**	They
29	**A**	positions	**B**	distances	**C**	areas	**D**	backgrounds
30	**A**	times	**B**	hours	**C**	ages	**D**	days
31	**A**	off	**B**	down	**C**	out	**D**	up
32	**A**	shouldn't	**B**	needn't	**C**	mustn't	**D**	wouldn't
33	**A**	quite	**B**	so	**C**	rather	**D**	very
34	**A**	unless	**B**	although	**C**	because	**D**	if
35	**A**	true	**B**	actual	**C**	normal	**D**	real

Advice

26 photos – *countable or uncountable?*

28 *Who is the teacher talking about? The camera, the students, the photos or the Earth?*

32 *They wanted the balloon to go higher, but they thought that it probably …*

34 *The balloon had travelled a long way, but it still worked!*

Test 2 Training — Writing Part 1

- How many pairs of sentences do you need to read?
- What do you need to do to the *second* sentence in the pair?

Grammar Comparing

1 🎧 30 Listen to Tom and Harry comparing two films. Which of the following was better in each film? Tick (✔) the correct film.

	Spaceship	Racers
the music	☐	☐
the acting	☐	☐
the costumes	☐	☐
the special effects	☐	☐
the action	☐	☐

2 Complete the second sentence in each pair so it means the same as the first.

Example   The music in *Racers* was worse than in *Spaceship*.
      Spaceship had **better music than** *Racers*.

1   The acting in *Racers* was better than in *Spaceship*.
   The acting in *Spaceship* wasn't .... in *Racers*.

2   The costumes in *Spaceship* weren't as colourful as in *Racers*.
   The costumes in *Racers* were .... than in *Spaceship*.

3   Harry liked the special effects in *Spaceship* more than in *Racers*.
   Harry .... the special effects in *Spaceship* to those in *Racers*.

4   Harry and Tom both agreed there was more action in *Racers*.
   Harry and Tom both agreed there wasn't .... action in *Spaceship*.

5   They haven't seen such a good film as *Racers* for a while.
   Racers is the .... film they've seen for a while.

3 Write the comparative form of these adjectives. Check your spelling carefully.

Example   big **bigger**   expensive **more expensive**

1 cheap ....   4 pretty ....   7 colourful ....
2 safe ....   5 crowded ....   8 busy ....
3 exciting ....   6 noisy ....   9 lively ....

> **Remember!**
> You add *-er* to short adjectives when comparing, and put *more* in front of longer adjectives, e.g. *more beautiful than*. There are some exceptions, e.g. *good / better* and *bad / worse*.

👁 PET candidates often make mistakes with *much* and *many*.

4 Find and correct the mistake in each sentence.

1   In a city, you'd have much more thing to do. ....
2   I haven't many time to read. ....
3   It's expensive and you can't see much people. ....
4   How much pairs of trousers have you got? ....
5   In Qatar there are many place if you want to go shopping. ....

Test 2 Exam practice — Writing • Part 1

Questions 1 – 5

Here are some sentences about learning English.
For each question, complete the second sentence so that it means the same as the first.
Use no more than three words.
Write only the missing words on your answer sheet.

> **Tip!** Make sure you don't leave anything out of the second sentence – it could change the meaning.

Example:

0   I first had English lessons when I started secondary school.

I've had English lessons ………………………… I started secondary school.

Answer: | 0 | since |

---

1   There are more letters to learn in my language than in English.

There aren't ………………………… letters to learn in English as in my language.

2   I've borrowed some very useful English books from my older brother.

My brother ………………………… me some very useful English books.

3   My teacher recently asked me if I wanted to join the after-school English club.

My teacher said, 'Do ………………………… join the after-school English club?'

4   I'm really good at speaking English now.

I can speak English really ………………………… now.

5   It can be hard to learn English without a teacher.

It can be hard to learn English ………………………… you don't have a teacher.

> **Advice**
>
> *1* How do we use **as ... as**?
>
> *2* If I borrow from you, you ... to me. Remember to keep the same tense as the original.

Test 2 Training — Writing Part 2

- How many words must your message be in length?
- How many points should it contain?

Grammar: Present perfect and past simple

1 When do we use the present perfect? Match the sentences with the descriptions a–c below.

1 I've lived in this house since 2009.   2 I've been to New York several times.   3 I've just had my hair cut!

a to talk about something that's recently happened, where we can still see the result
b to talk about something that started in the past and is still continuing
c to talk about past experiences, no definite time

2 (CD 1 31) Complete Jake and Maria's conversation about school trips with the correct tense of the verbs in brackets. Then listen and check your answers.

Jake: Well, we **(0)** ...'ve had... (have) some great school trips this year, haven't we?
Maria: You're right! Remember the trip to the museum? That **(1)** .... (be) great! I **(2)** .... (never see) so many paintings in my life!
Jake: And we **(3)** .... (go) to a great place at the start of term, too – the weather forecasting station.
Maria: Yes, we **(4)** .... (learn) a lot that day. That **(5)** .... (be) a while ago. But we still **(6)** .... (not visit) the sports centre. I hope we do.
Jake: Mmm. We **(7)** .... (not go) to the Botanic Gardens yet either.
Maria: Oh, I **(8)** .... (already go) there. My father **(9)** .... (take) me last year.

> **Remember!**
> These words are often used with the present perfect: *how long…?, ever, never, just, already, yet, since, for.*
> Use the past simple to talk about actions and events in the past that have finished.

3 Complete the sentences with *been* or *gone*.

1 Why don't we go to the pool this weekend?
No, we've .... there loads of times.
2 Is Mum at home?
No, she's .... to pick Dad up from work.

> **Remember!**
> Use **have been** as the present perfect of *go* to mean *went and came back again*, e.g. *Where's John? – He's gone to the shop.* (and he's still there) but *You're late! – Sorry! I've been to the dentist.* (but I'm back now).

Writing Part 2

4 Write the past participles for these common verbs.

1 write .... 5 eat .... 9 lose ....
2 drive .... 6 steal .... 10 shine ....
3 drink .... 7 choose .... 11 break ....
4 wear .... 8 swim .... 12 ride ....

> **Tip!** If you're not sure of some verbs, check the Verbs page at the back of your book. Aim to learn a few of them regularly.

◉ PET candidates often make mistakes with present perfect and past simple forms.

5 Cross out and correct the mistake in each sentence.

1 I **have read** your letter ten minutes ago, and I've decided to write to you immediately. ....
2 Recently my room **looks** untidy. ....
3 Last month a new shop **has opened**, and they have very nice trousers, shoes and shirts. ....
4 I will tell you about the restaurant that **had just opened** in our town. ....
5 Klaus **is** in the club for thirty years and he is really well trained. ....
6 Last year I **have been** camping with my parents and it was great. ....

Test 2 Exam practice — Writing • Part 2

Question 6

You are helping to organise an end-of-term party for your class. Your friend Ben has just come back from his holiday and has forgotten all about the party.
Write an email to Ben. In your email you should:

- remind Ben about when the party is

- tell Ben what you are doing to prepare for the party

- arrange to take Ben to the party with you.

Write **35–45 words** on your answer sheet.

> **Tip!** Make sure you write about all *three* points in your answer.
>
> **Advice**
>
> **remind** Think about how to remind someone about something, e.g. **Don't forget ...**
>
> **tell** What things do you need to do to prepare for a party? Some ideas: buy food, organise some music, invite friends.
>
> **arrange** What might you suggest? Pick him up / take him with you in your parents' car / go together on the bus?

Test 2 Training — Writing Part 3

- You can choose between two different types of writing – what are they?
- How many words do you have to write?

Focus Planning

1 Write down a few words for a composition on one of these topics.

  a your town
  b your favourite sport
  c getting an email from a friend you haven't seen recently
  d playing in a school concert

Tip! You won't have time to write a detailed plan for your work in the exam, but just a few words may be enough.

Grammar -ing forms

2 Circle the correct verb form to complete each sentence.

  1 I'd like *to go / going* to the cinema tonight.
  2 I'm interested in *to visit / visiting* new places.
  3 Are you any good at *to take / taking* photos?
  4 I don't mind *to help / helping* in the kitchen when my mum's busy.
  5 My friends and I all enjoy *to meet / meeting* new people at parties.
  6 I don't want *to do / doing* my homework all weekend.

Remember! When a verb follows a preposition, it takes the *-ing* form, e.g. *I'm good at swimming. I'm interested in learning to cook. I'm worried about spending too much money. I'm looking forward to having a break.*
Some verbs in English are followed by an *-ing* form and some are followed by *to* + infinitive. You need to learn how different verbs are used.

👁 PET candidates often make mistakes with *-ing* forms.

3 Cross out and correct the mistake in each sentence.

  1 If you're **interested in to visit** historic buildings, you should go to Rome. ....
  2 I can **go to swimming** every Saturday. ....
  3 I was **afraid of to miss** the bus. ....
  4 You **can dancing, drinking and singing** there. ....
  5 Now it's winter and you **must wearing** very warm clothes. ....

4 Imagine you're writing a letter in which you have to describe yourself. What would you say – the kind of person you are? the sort of things you are good at doing? your plans for the future? Write down some ideas and then talk with your partner.

Spelling Adding *-ing* to verbs

5 Write the correct *-ing* form for these verbs.

1 shop	6 put	11 chat ....
2 get	7 travel	12 forget ....
3 cut	8 set	13 begin ....
4 stop	9 win	14 sit ....
5 shut	10 drop	15 run ....

6 Write the correct *-ing* form for these verbs. Check your spelling carefully.

1 take	8 fly	15 carry ....
2 write	9 listen	16 hope ....
3 save	10 come	17 lie ....
4 choose	11 use	18 hide ....
5 eat	12 enjoy	19 cycle ....
6 make	13 buy	20 go ....
7 study	14 smile	

Remember!

When you add *-ing* to some verbs, you need to double the middle letter in some of them, e.g. *run – ru**nn**ing*, *begin – begi**nn**ing*.

For other verbs that end in *-e*, drop the final *-e* before adding *-ing*, e.g. *make – making*.

Verbs that end in *-ie* change to a *-y*, e.g. *lie – lying*.

Focus Punctuation

7a Look at the passage below about Mark and his new bicycle. Try reading it aloud. Add full stops and capital letters then read it again.

Mark got a new bicycle for his birthday he was so thrilled that he took it outside immediately he rode it up and down the street until he got bored and decided he needed to try it out somewhere else just then his friend Jack arrived he suggested they took their bikes to the park Mark thought that was a good idea so off they went at the park they set up some jumps and rode their bikes right over them all day Mark's new bike got covered in mud but he had a brilliant time

Tips! It's important to punctuate your work clearly when you're writing – it helps the reader understand what you want to say.

Reading your work aloud can help you decide where the full stops should go.

b Look at the passage again. You could also break it into three paragraphs. Where would each one begin?

Remember!

Start a new paragraph for a new topic – new time, new place, new action, new speaker.

Test 2 Exam practice — Writing • Part 3

Write an answer to **one** of the questions (**7** or **8**) in this part.
Write your answer in about **100 words** on your answer sheet.

Tip! Leave yourself time to check through your work when you've finished writing.
Before you start writing, look at both questions and see which one you could say more about. You don't have time to change your mind after you've started.

Question 7

- This is part of a letter you receive from a new English penfriend, Jo.

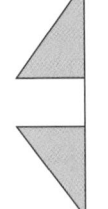

> So that's all about me. Tell me all about yourself! What do you like doing in your spare time? And what do you like best about your studies?

- Now write a letter to Jo, answering the questions.
- Write your **letter** on your answer sheet.

Question 8

- Your English teacher has asked you to write a story.
- Your story must begin with this sentence:

    Sarah knew the present from her friend was the best she had ever received!

- Write your **story** on your answer sheet.

Advice

7 Think about your spare time – sport? music? TV? shopping? reading? seeing friends?

What do you like about your studies? maths? English? science? art? your school? your teachers? being with your friends?

8 What was the present? Who was the friend? Why did the friend buy it? Why was it such a good present for Sarah?

Test 2 Training — Listening Part 1

- How many short recordings do you listen to?
- How many people could be speaking in each one?

Grammar Pronouns

1 🎧 32 Read what Tim says about his teacher. Where necessary, replace the underlined section with one of these pronouns. Then listen and check your answers.

> they   we   he   them   us   his

The teacher, Mr Lyons, said my classmates and I had to do more homework if (1) <u>my classmates and I</u> wanted to succeed in (2) <u>Mr Lyons'</u> class, so (3) <u>Mr Lyons</u> gave (4) <u>my classmates and me</u> some really tough exercises. (5) <u>The really tough exercises</u> were so difficult that even my big sister Gail, who's very clever, couldn't do (6) <u>the really tough exercises</u>. But in the end (7) <u>Mr Lyons</u> showed us how to do (8) <u>the really tough exercises</u> and (9) <u>my classmates and I</u> all got high marks. (10) <u>Mr Lyons</u> was very happy with (11) <u>my classmates and me</u>!

Tip! You sometimes need to understand reference words (*him, her, it, this, that*) to follow what the speakers are talking about.

Remember! When speakers are talking, they don't always repeat the name of the person or thing they are talking about. They use pronouns instead, for example *him, her, we, us, his, he, they, them*. It's important to know what these are replacing in a text.

👁 PET candidates often make mistakes with pronouns.

2 Cross out and correct the mistake in each sentence.
1. I like wildlife, so I always watch programmes about **them**. ....
2. Last week I bought **me** a pair of jeans. ....
3. I asked **he** what had happened. ....
4. Take care of **you**! ....
5. It was a nice idea of **you** to remember your old friend. ....
6. He told **she** that the suitcase could be in the attic. ....

Remember! You may also need to use reflexive pronouns.
I – myself   we – ourselves
you – yourself   you (pl) – yourselves
he – himself   they – themselves
her – herself

3 Look at the three pictures below. What kind of programme is each TV showing? Which one would *you* watch?

A   B   C

4a 🎧 33 What will the boy watch on TV tonight? Listen and choose A, B or C.

Tip! Understanding pronouns can help you get the answer.

b Listen again. Look at the underlined words below. What is the boy talking about?
1. I love <u>those</u>.
2. We'll probably end up watching <u>that</u>.
3. I don't want you to miss <u>it</u>.

Test 2 Exam practice — Listening • Part 1

Questions 1 – 7

There are seven questions in this part.
For each question, choose the correct answer (**A**, **B** or **C**).

Tip! Underline important words in the question so that you know what you're listening for before the recording begins.

Example: What did the boy forget to bring home from school?

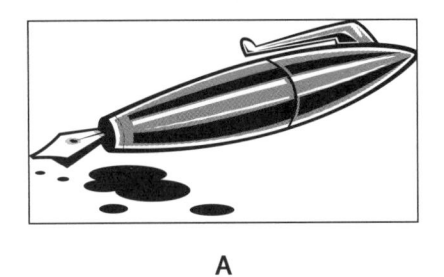

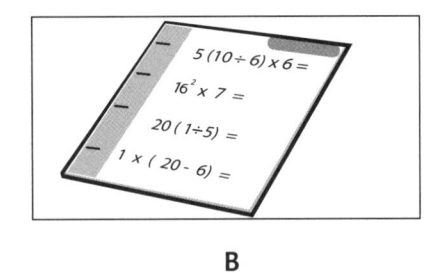

A   B   C (circled)

---

1 How did the boy get to the cinema?

A   B   C

> **Advice**
>
> **1** The boy says the bus **broke down** – so was it possible to travel on it? Where was the boy's dad? Why has the boy got his bike with him?

2 What did the girl see on her holiday?

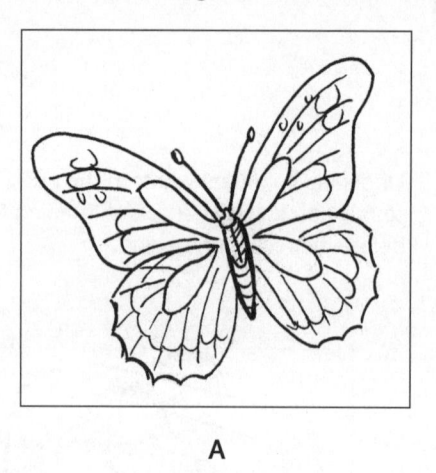

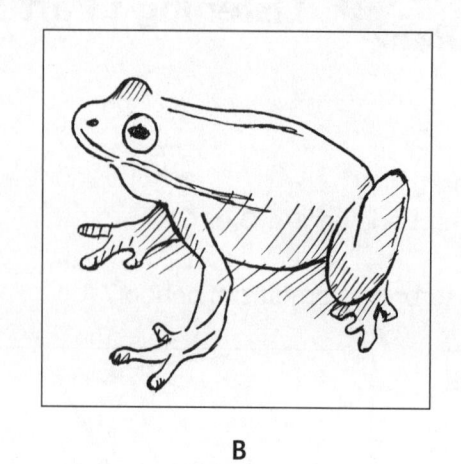

A   B   C

3 Which instrument will the girl play in the concert?

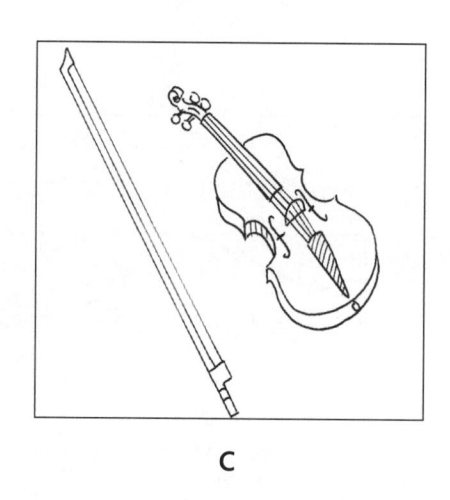

A   B   C

4 What does the boy want to cook for tonight's meal?

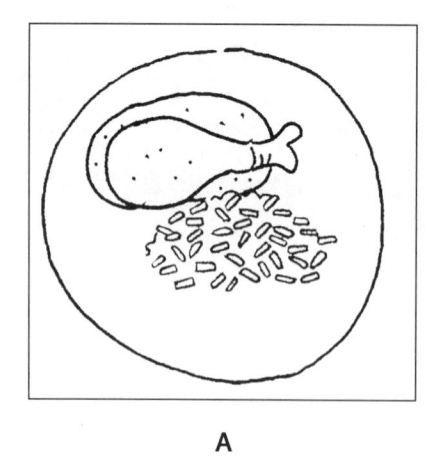

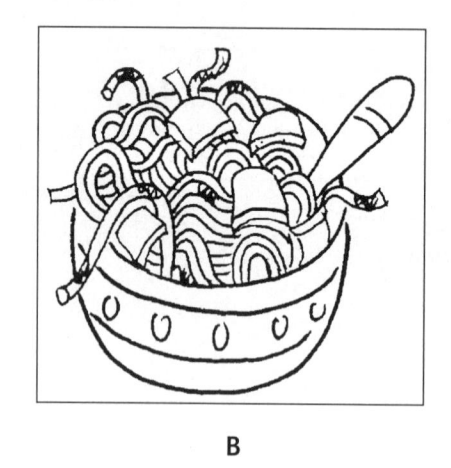

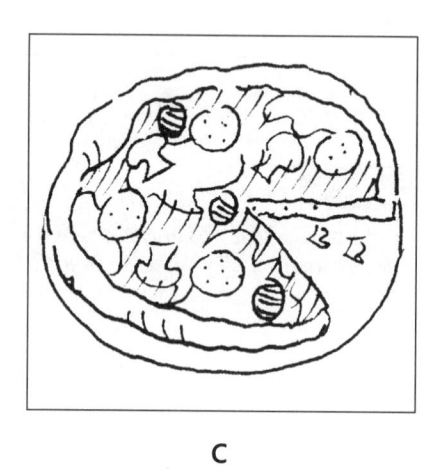

A   B   C

78 | Test 2 Exam practice

Listening Part 1

5 Where will they meet?

A   B   C

6 What will the boy buy?

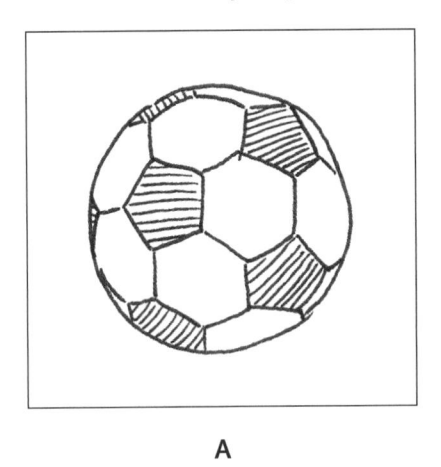

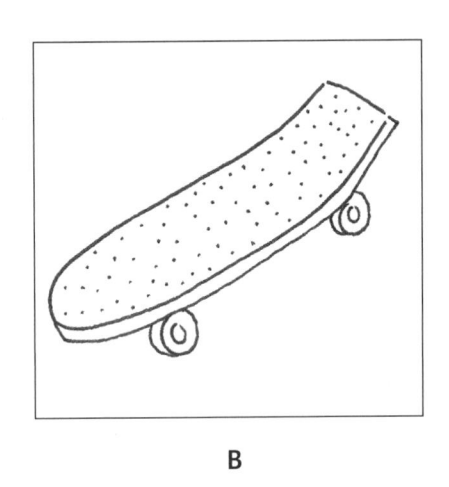

A   B   C

7 Where is the girl's older brother at the moment?

A   B   C

Advice

5 What are the **three** things that the boy tells the girl about the library?

6 Which one does the boy **need** to buy?

Listening Part 1

Test 2 Training — Listening Part 2

- How many people do you listen to in the recording?
- What kind of questions do you have to answer?

1 Sarah and Peter are going on an outdoor adventure trip with their classmates next week. What will they find enjoyable? What will be difficult for them? In pairs, look at the list and talk about each idea.

> feeling cold   being part of a team   sailing
> being away from home   eating outdoors   feeling exhausted
> sleeping in a tent   climbing steep rocks

Grammar Future forms

2 Match each sentence about the future with the correct meaning.

1 My team will definitely win the football match!
2 I'm going to watch TV when I get home.
3 I'm meeting Kris in town at 6 p.m.
4 Hmm – I think I'll call in and see Alex on the way home.

a It's something you've already decided and arranged to do, maybe with another person.
b It's something you predict will happen.
c It's something you intend to do yourself.
d It's a decision you're making as you speak.

Tip! Listen carefully to the text – sometimes choosing the right option depends on understanding the tenses the speaker is using.

Remember! Check that you can recognise other words that might be used to talk about the future, e.g. *shall, shan't, won't, might, planning to, expecting to, hoping to, would like to*. You may need to match these with one of the options in Part 2.

3 🎧 35 Listen to Sarah talking about what she's going to do tomorrow. Choose the correct answer A or B for each question.

1 When is Sarah going to get up?
   A earlier than usual
   B at the normal time

2 What is Sarah doing tomorrow?
   A travelling into town with a friend
   B seeing someone she knows in town

3 What does Sarah think she'll do in town?
   A see a film
   B go to the library

4 What will the weather be like, according to Sarah's mum?
   A fine
   B wet

5 What is Sarah going to do when she gets home?
   A read a book
   B spend time in the garden

6 What is Sarah's mum doing tomorrow afternoon?
   A making tea for her friend
   B visiting a friend

Test 2 Exam practice — Listening • Part 2

CD 1 36 Questions 8 – 13

You will hear an interview with a girl called Maria Shaw, who went on an outdoor adventure trip with girls from her school. For each question, choose the correct answer **A**, **B** or **C**.

Tip! The options may not repeat the exact words of the text, so read each option carefully as you're listening to the text.

8 Maria didn't think she'd find the trip hard because
   A she'd had experience of camping with her family.
   B she'd always cycled a long way to school every day.
   C she'd been on walking trips with the school.

Advice
9 What was Maria afraid she <u>wouldn't</u> do?
10 What took them time when they were climbing?

9 What was Maria worried about during the first day's activities?
   A She wouldn't complete everything in time.
   B She'd be very cold while she was there.
   C She wouldn't manage to sail in the right direction.

10 What made the climb up the rocks so slow?
   A The group kept slipping on the slopes.
   B Several students fell and hurt themselves.
   C Parts of the climb were extremely steep.

11 When Maria's group got to the top of the rocks, they
   A were given a talk on the environment.
   B took photos of each other.
   C ate a big meal.

12 Maria says that by the end of the trip the girls were
   A feeling keen to go home again.
   B working together better.
   C cooking food for each other.

13 What will Maria do for her next trip?
   A take her family with her
   B spend time on a beach
   C go somewhere with wilder countryside

Test 2 Training   Listening Part 3

- How many speakers do you listen to in Part 3?
- What kind of words do you need to write in the gaps in the notes?

Focus Numbers and letters

1 🎧 37 **How do you say these numbers and letters? Listen and repeat.**

1 23 April
2 1,260
3 13 km
4 J-A-Y-B-U-R-Y
5 1967
6 2nd
7 30th July
8 F-E-B-R-U-A-R-Y
9 www.redflight.com

Tip! In this part of the test, be ready to write down different numbers and spellings.

2 🎧 38 **Listen and write what you hear.**

1 a date: ....
2 a year: ....
3 a distance: ....
4 a website: ....
5 a length of time: ....
6 a time: ....
7 a name: ....
8 a telephone number: ....

Remember!
Here are some examples of what you may hear in dates or websites and have to write. Do you know how to say them? Check with your teacher.
dot   com   1st   2nd   3rd   4th   5th
20th   21st   30th   31st

Focus Spellings

3 Work in pairs. Spell out the names of some people you know. Your partner writes them down and tries to guess who each person is. Use the ideas below, or your own ideas.

your uncle	your sports coach
your aunt	a sports team member
a famous singer	your best friend
your cousin	your music teacher
an actor	a musician

4 Look at these words which people often misspell. First <u>look</u> at each one carefully and <u>say</u> it. Then <u>cover</u> each one in turn with a sheet of paper and <u>write</u> it. Finally <u>check</u>, is it correct? If it isn't, cover it and try again.

Tip! In Part 3 it's important to try to spell correctly the words you write down in the notes. Use the steps *Look, say, cover, write, check*.

Tip! Collect difficult words of your own. Think about keeping the words you find difficult in a notebook – your own personal dictionary!

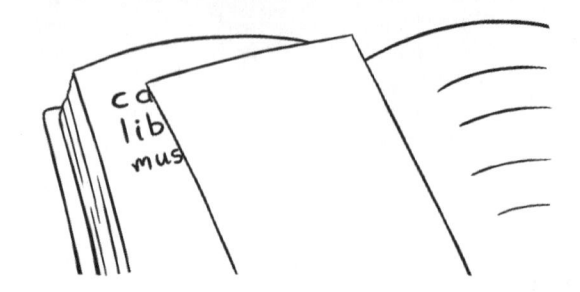

	First try	Second try
castle	*castel*	*castle*
library	....	....
museum	....	....

> PET candidates often make spelling mistakes.

5 Each word in the list is spelt incorrectly. Write the correct spelling.

1 wheather	7 castel	13 neightbour	19 diffrent ....
2 sighseeing	8 clouthes	14 tought	20 libery ....
3 coffe	9 begining	15 interessting	21 tomorrw ....
4 coutry	10 meusem	16 belive	22 becase ....
5 adress	11 clases	17 resturant	23 tipical ....
6 hollidays	12 mountins	18 wich	24 recive ....

Test 2 Exam practice — Listening • Part 3

🎧 39 **Questions 14 – 19**

You will hear a boy called Josh talking to his class about a trip he recently went on.
For each question, fill in the missing information in the numbered spaces.

Tip! In your answer, you don't need to change the word or words you hear.

JOSH'S WEATHER CENTRE TRIP

Josh went to the Weather Centre with his **(14)** ....

Josh says the Centre first reported strong winds in **(15)** ....

The Centre later put forecasts in **(16)** .... for everyone to see.

Lots of weather information now comes from **(17)** ...., according to Josh.

Josh thinks people need to know how much **(18)** .... there'll be.

Josh says that his local **(19)** .... always needs to know about the weather.

Advice

15 Listen and write down a _year_.

16 _Where_ can people read information every day?

18 What kind of _bad_ weather will people need to know about?

Test 2 Training — Listening Part 4

- What type of conversation will you listen to?
- How many statements do you have to look at?

Focus Positive and negative opinions

1 Look at these ways of giving opinions about a holiday. Which ones are positive (P) and which are negative (N)?

1 I can't wait to go! ....
2 I'm not that keen on holidays. ....
3 I'm really looking forward to it! ....
4 I've heard the place is awful. ....

Tip! It's important to listen carefully to both speakers in the recording and identify whether their attitude or opinion is *positive* or *negative*.

2a 🎧 40 Listen to Paulo talking about a holiday he's going on soon with his family and his older brother Jack. Is he positive or negative about these things? Tick the correct box.

1 going surfing
2 Jack coming too
3 Jack having the biggest room
4 Jack playing football with Paulo
5 Jack paying for Paulo's windsurfing

b What expressions does Paolo use to show he's positive or negative?

Focus Agreeing and disagreeing

3 Look at what Paulo said after the holiday and the responses of his family. Did they agree (A) or disagree (D)?

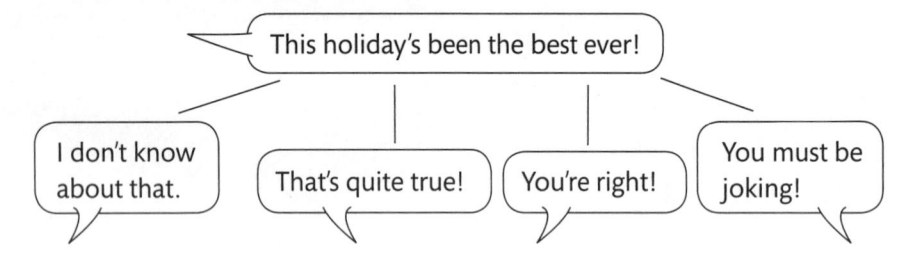

This holiday's been the best ever!

- I don't know about that.
- That's quite true!
- You're right!
- You must be joking!

Remember!
Agreeing and disagreeing
I agree with you.   Maybe, but …
I know what you mean.   Actually, I don't think so. I think …
I think so, too.   I'm afraid I don't agree.

4 In pairs, write down other ways of agreeing and disagreeing.

5 Do you agree or disagree with these sentences? Write answers then compare with a partner.

1 Staying at home and watching a film on TV is much better than going to the cinema.
2 You can learn more from reading a book than playing a computer game.
3 Wearing a school uniform is much easier than having to decide what to wear every day.
4 Swimming outdoors in the sea or a river is much nicer than swimming indoors in a pool.

Test 2 Exam practice — Listening • Part 4

Questions 20 – 25

Look at the six sentences for this part.
You will hear a girl, Anna, and a boy, Harry, talking about heroes.
Decide if each sentence is correct or incorrect.
If it is correct, choose the letter **A** for **YES**. If it is not correct,
choose the letter **B** for **NO**.

Tip! If the sentence is about what the speakers both think, make sure you listen carefully to both speakers before you choose your answer.

		YES	NO
20	Harry disagrees that Superman is a good example of a modern-day hero.	A	B
21	Anna thinks a hero has to be someone who does brave things.	A	B
22	Harry wishes people like his grandfather were recognised for what they do.	A	B
23	Anna agrees with Harry that without heroes, story books would be less interesting.	A	B
24	Anna's discovered lots of writers who have made her want to read.	A	B
25	They've both found examples of heroes to admire among famous people.	A	B

Advice

20 What does Harry say about what lots of people think? How about what **he** thinks?

21 What does Anna suggest about heroes? Do they always do brave things?

22 Does Harry think his grandfather is a hero? Is his grandfather famous?

Test 2 Training — Speaking Part 1

- Who do you have to talk to?
- How long do you have to talk?

1 Match the names used for the people involved in the Speaking Test with the people in the photo.

> the candidates   an interlocutor (who asks the questions)
> an assessor (who doesn't speak during the test)

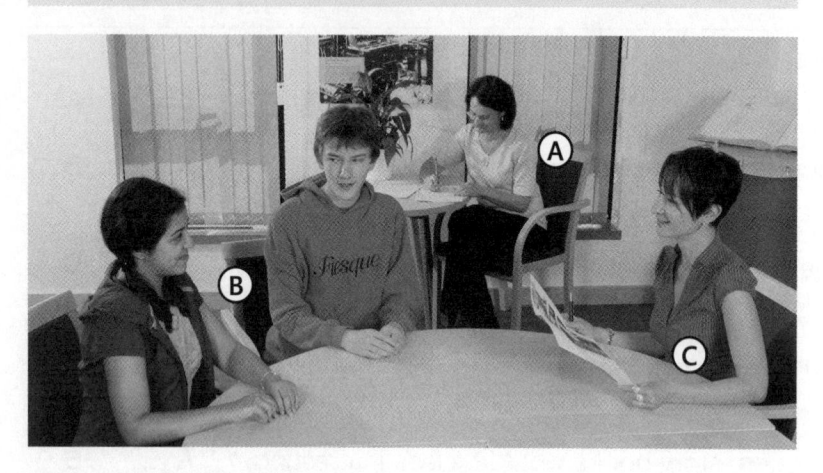

Tip! You will need to respond to questions about present circumstances, past experiences and future plans.

Focus General questions

2 Look at the kind of questions that the interlocutor might ask you. Note down the answers you would give.

1. What's your surname?
2. How do you spell it?
3. Where do you live?
4. Do you study English at school?
5. How long have you studied English?
6. What do you enjoy doing at school?
7. Tell me about your home.
8. What did you do last weekend?

Tip! The interlocutor will ask you to spell your name in English. Be prepared.

Tip! For questions 3–8 try to give more than one-word answers whenever you can.

3 🎧 42 Listen to a boy called Jake asking a girl called Melissa the questions in exercise 2. Tick (✔) Right or Wrong.

	Right	Wrong
1 Melissa's surname is spelt J-A-D-F-U-W-A-N.	☐	☐
2 Melissa lives near North Park.	☐	☐
3 She doesn't think she's very good at English.	☐	☐
4 Melissa has had English lessons for about five years.	☐	☐
5 Melissa enjoys the lunch she has at school.	☐	☐
6 Melissa lives in a first-floor flat.	☐	☐
7 The place she lives is quite quiet.	☐	☐
8 Melissa's home has a garden.	☐	☐
9 Melissa has three sisters.	☐	☐
10 Melissa saw her grandparents last weekend.	☐	☐

Tip! Practise talking about your daily routine, likes and dislikes but also practise asking your partner for information on these topics.

Test 2 Exam practice — Speaking • Part 1

(2–3 minutes)

Phase 1
Interlocutor

A/B Good morning / afternoon / evening.
Can I have your marksheets, please?
(Hand over the marksheets to the Assessor)

A/B I'm .... (name) and this is my colleague .... (name).
He / she is just going to listen to us.

A Now, what's your name?
Thank you.

B And what's your name?
Thank you.

B Candidate B, what's your surname?
How do you spell it?
Thank you.

A And, Candidate A, what's your surname?
How do you spell it?
Thank you.

A/B
- Where do you live / come from?
- Do you study English at school?
- Do you like it?
- Thank you.

- Do you live in ...?
- Do you have English lessons?

Phase 2
Interlocutor

Tip! Try to answer the phase 2 questions with two or three sentences joined together.

(The interlocutor may ask one or more of the following questions.)

What's your favourite school subject? Why?

Tell us about one of your teachers.

What do you like doing at the weekends?

Tell us about the area where you live.

Thank you.

Advice

Phase 1 I like studying English because ... (e.g. **it's interesting / I can talk to a lot of different people ...**)

Phase 2 Don't forget **like + -ing** (e.g. **I like going to the cinema and meeting my friends.**). What other verbs of liking do you know? e.g. **I quite like ... I enjoy ... I love ...**

Test 2 Training — Speaking Part 2

- Who will you talk with?
- You will be given something to talk about. What will it be?

Focus Interacting with a partner

1 In Part 2 of the test you will need to discuss a topic with your partner. To do this, you will need to show that you can do the following. Put the expressions below under the correct heading.

Tip! Make sure you show interest in what your partner is saying. Try to respond to what they say.

agree	disagree	give reasons	make suggestions	ask for opinions

How about you?   You're right.   I'm not sure about that.   Let's ...   I think so too.   Do you agree?
That's a great idea.   That's not such a good idea.   Why don't we ...?   ... because ...   ... so that ...
What do you think about ...?   That's a good idea, isn't it?   What if ...?

2 🎧 43 Listen to Kevin and Jasmine talking about advertising a school concert and complete the conversation. Their teacher has suggested the following ways of letting people know about the concert.

posters around the town   emails to parents
notices in school   leaflets to pupils

Kevin: Hi Jasmine. So (0) ......*Let's*...... talk about how we can let people know about our school concert.

Jasmine: OK. (1) .... putting up posters? That's a good idea, (2) ....?

Kevin: (3) .... about that (4) .... we'd need to have them made – that could cost a lot. (5) .... writing something on the computer instead? Do (6) ....?

Jasmine: (7) .... – our teacher could check it and then we can print it. Oh, but (8) .... everyone takes them home and then forgets to give them to their parents?

Kevin: Oh, (9) .... OK, (10) .... ask our teacher if she'll send out emails to parents.

Jasmine: Yes, and we can also put a few notices around school.

3 Talk with your partner about what makes a successful school concert that everyone will enjoy. Think about the following ideas for the concert.

classical music   pop bands   a play   a musical

Remember! You will need to keep this discussion going for two to three minutes.

Tip! If you have time, try to summarise the reasons for your final choice at the end of Part 2.

Test 2 Exam practice — Speaking • Part 2

(2–3 minutes)

Tip! Remember to look at your partner in this part when you're speaking – not the interlocutor.

Interlocutor
(to both candidates)

> I'm going to describe a situation to you.
>
> You are members of a local **youth club**. The club wants to advertise a **party** for club members, and the leader has decided to ask you to help **make posters** to put around the club. Talk together about the **different** things you could use to make the posters, and then decide which things would be the **best** to use.
>
> Here is a picture with some ideas to help you.

*Place **Test 2 Exam practice Speaking Part 2** picture (see page C2) in front of candidates.*

> I'll say that again.
>
> You are members of a local **youth club**. The club wants to advertise a **party** for club members, and the leader has decided to ask you to help **make posters** to put around the club. Talk together about the **different** things you could use to make the posters, and then decide which things would be the **best** to use.

> All right? Talk together.

Allow the candidates enough time to complete the task without interruption. Prompt only if necessary.

> Thank you. (Can I have the booklet please?)

🎧 44 **Listen to two students doing the task above.**

Test 2 Training   Speaking Part 3

(3 minutes)

- You will be given something to talk about. What will it be?

Focus Describing photos

1. In pairs, choose one photo each. Tell your partner what you can see in your photo. Speak for about a minute.

   Tip! You will need to speak for approximately a minute.

   A

   B

2. Look at your photos again and describe them as thoroughly as you can. Think about the following:

   - Who are the people?
   - Where are they?
   - What are they doing?
   - Why are they doing this?
   - What are they wearing?
   - What can you see in the background?
   - What's the weather like?
   - What season is it?

   Tip! Don't worry if you don't know the word for something in the photo. Try to keep talking.

   Tip! Some simple words and phrases like *behind*, *in front of* and *next to* can be useful for describing the photo.

   Remember! You have to talk on your own about what you can see in a photograph.

   🎧 45 Listen to a student talking about Photo A.

   🎧 46 Listen to a student talking about Photo B.

Test 2 Exam practice Speaking • Part 3

(3 minutes)

Tip! Don't worry if you don't know the word for something in the picture you are given – use the language you <u>do</u> know to find a way around it.

Interlocutor
(to both candidates)

Now I'd like both of you to talk on your own about something. I'm going to give both of you a photograph of **teenagers doing sports**.

Candidate A, here is your photograph. Please show it to Candidate B, but I'd like you to talk about it.

*Place **Test 2 Exam practice Speaking Part 3** picture (see page C7) in front of Candidate A.*

Candidate B, you just listen. I'll give you your photograph in a moment.

(Candidate A)

(Approximately 1 minute)

If there is a need to intervene, prompts rather than direct questions should be used.

Thank you.

Interlocutor

Now, Candidate B, here is your photograph. It also shows **people playing sports**. Please show it to Candidate A, and tell us what you can see in the photograph.

*Place **Test 2 Exam practice Speaking Part 3** picture (see page C8) in front of Candidate B.*

(Candidate B)

(Approximately 1 minute)

Thank you.

🎧 47 **Listen to a student talking about Photo A.**

🎧 48 **Listen to a student talking about Photo B.**

Test 2 Training Speaking Part 4

(3 minutes)
- Who will you talk to in this part?
- What will you talk about?

Focus Question forms

1 Below are different ways to begin questions in English. Match the question beginnings and endings.

1	What do you	a	been to a gym in your town?
2	Are you	b	swim when you were five?
3	Are you good at	c	a swimming pool near your home?
4	Can you	d	watch any sport next weekend?
5	Could you	e	do to keep fit?
6	Are you going to	f	like to try a new sport?
7	Would you	g	interested in football?
8	Is there	h	snowboarding or skiing?
9	Have you ever	i	run three kilometres without stopping?

Tip! If you run out of things to say, ask your partner a question about the topic to keep the conversation going.

2 Work with a partner and ask each other the questions above.

Vocabulary Health and fitness

3 Look at the ways of giving your opinion and giving a reason below. Ask what your partner thinks about health and fitness. What should you do if you want to stay fit and healthy? What shouldn't you do? Try to give a reason for your opinion. Use the ideas in the box to help you.

> go to a gym   go jogging   eat chocolate
> play computer games   eat fruit and vegetables   walk to school
> eat fast food   go to bed early

Opinion
*I think you should …   You shouldn't …   I don't think you should …
You don't have to …*

Reason
*I think you should go to a gym to do exercise **because** there's someone there to give you advice.*

4 Now talk together about the sports you like and don't like doing at school, and say why.

Tip! Involve your partner and ask for their opinions.

Test 2 Exam practice — Speaking • Part 4

(3 minutes)

Tip! Invite your partner to join in the conversation – don't do all the talking yourself.

Interlocutor
(to both candidates)

> Your photographs showed **teenagers doing sport**, alone and in a team. Now I'd like you to talk together about the kind of sports and activities **you** enjoy when you're **not** at school and **why** you like doing them.

Allow the candidates enough time to complete the task without intervention. Prompt only if necessary.

> Thank you. That's the end of the test.

🎧 49 **Listen to some additional questions on this topic and give your answers.**

1. Do you prefer watching sport or taking part?
2. Which sporting events do you enjoy watching? What about your family?
3. Do you prefer to be part of a team like in football, or do solo sports like skateboarding?
4. What else do you do to try to stay fit and healthy?

Advice

Don't forget to use expressions of agreeing / disagreeing / asking for opinions.

How many ways do you know to ask your partner questions?
e.g. **What do you usually ...? Do you ...? Do you like ...? Can you ...? Have you ever ...?**

Test 3 Reading • Part 1

Questions 1 – 5

Look at the text in each question.
What does it say?
Mark the correct letter **A**, **B** or **C** on your answer sheet.

Example:

0

Class 8T – History lesson

Miss Wade asks you to read pages 25–30 of your textbook and do task on 'transport' for homework – to hand in next Monday – as she's ill today.

A Miss Wade wants Class 8T to help her arrange transport for next Monday.

B Class 8T have work to get on with while their teacher is absent.

C Anyone in Class 8T who is ill today can hand in their homework next week.

Answer: 0 A **B** C

1

Carrie, I won't be home until 6 p.m. Have the snack I've left for you and Josh and then I'll cook dinner when I get home. Love Mum

Carrie's mum wants

A Carrie to get dinner ready for her and Josh by 6 p.m.

B Carrie not to give Josh anything to eat until she arrives home.

C Carrie and Josh to eat something before they have dinner.

2

**Students – keep to the left!
Running in the corridor is forbidden at all times.**

A Students cannot use this corridor to go the sports hall.

B Students must never run along the corridor.

C Students on the right side of the corridor are permitted to walk quickly.

3

> Anyone wanting to be in the school play
> this term should
> give their name to Mrs Walters
> by the end of the week.

A Mrs Walters wants to know the names of the students performing this week.

B Students hoping to act in the play need to tell Mrs Walters this week.

C Anyone wanting to see this term's play must get a ticket from Mrs Walters.

4

> Due to technical problems,
> this week's Film Club meeting
> is postponed until further notice

A The club meeting is cancelled for an unknown period because of faulty equipment.

B The meeting has been put off until next week when there'll be new equipment.

C Because of equipment problems this week's club meeting is delayed until tomorrow.

5

> **Students Support Recycling!**
> Get rid of your unwanted clothes
> Collection Monday morning – Main Hall

What should students do on Monday?

A Take anything they don't want to wear any more to the Main Hall.

B Go to a school uniform sale in the Main Hall.

C Collect all their old school clothes to take home with them.

Test 3 Reading • Part 2

Questions 6 – 10

The young people below all want to go to a science camp.
On the opposite page there are descriptions of eight science camps.
Decide which camp would be the most suitable for the following people.
For questions **6–10**, mark the correct letter (**A–H**) on your answer sheet.

6 Peter is 13 and wants to spend a day making model planes. He enjoys designing things and loves taking part in competitions.

7 Hamida is 12 and wants to spend about a week learning a variety of science topics. She's interested in space and would like to do some experiments.

8 Paulo is 17 and loves collecting rocks and shells. He's keen to spend a week outdoors with people his own age, finding out more about the things he collects.

9 Annie and Lisa are 11 and want to learn some simple experiments to show their families. They want to spend a day making friends in a small group.

10 Klaus is 15 and would like to be an astronaut one day, so he wants a week-long course where he can find out about the universe and how to explore it.

Eight Science Camps

A Socket to me!

This is a week-long camp for girls aged 11–15 on how to use computers. Students will also learn about how computers are changing our world and increasing our knowledge of the universe. There are sessions on building your own computer and basic programming.

B Super Camp

Students will get excited about all kinds of science over the six days of this camp. They'll learn how to test for water quality out in the field and spend time in the chemistry lab. After dark is the best time to look at the planets and our experts know all about black holes! For 11-to-13-year-olds.

C Chemistry Magic

Students need to sign up early as places on this interesting day course are limited to just six. Students, aged 10 to 12, will learn how to safely make different chemicals change colour, catch fire or glow in the dark! Parents are invited to come and see the 'magic tricks' the students have learned in a show at 3 p.m.

D On Target

Whose flying machine will stay in the air the longest? Whose will land closest to the target? On 19th November, a professional engineer will take 20 students aged between 11 and 14 through the whole design process to create their winning aircraft. There are prizes for the best design.

E Steps

This is a one-week introduction to a range of engineering design and technology topics for boys aged 13 to 15 only. And there'll be lots of opportunities to make new friends at different outdoor evening activities which include swimming and pizza parties.

F Star Camp

High-school students of 15 and over are welcome to question the experts on this course about anything from time travel to the life of stars and plenty of space-related topics in between. They will design and build a space rocket and visit museums and a telescope during their seven-day stay.

G Field Camp

This camp provides older teenagers with an understanding of how our planet works and what it's made of. From Sunday to Saturday students will sleep in tents in the desert and learn about how the mountains and valleys were made and useful things like reading a map and making a campfire.

H Maths into Design

This interesting and friendly day course mixes art and science and is a good introduction to maths and measurement for children aged 9 to 11. Students build a mathematical shape then have fun decorating it with their original art designs. They can then take their work home to show their families.

Reading • Part 3

Questions 11 – 20

Look at the sentences below about a sports event for young people.
Read the text on the opposite page to decide if each sentence is correct or incorrect.
If it is correct, mark **A** on your answer sheet.
If it is not correct, mark **B** on your answer sheet.

11 It is expected that some children will fail to complete the races in the triathlon.

12 There will be several triathlons held in the region this year.

13 Everyone taking part in races has to have an annual membership with OAT.

14 Athletes run, swim and cycle various distances, depending on their age.

15 It is possible to do the triathlon as part of a team.

16 Athletes need to collect their race bag the day before the main event.

17 Before the race, athletes need to check their bikes themselves.

18 People wanting to attend the 'clinic' on June 17th need to book and pay in advance.

19 Parents are welcome to help out on the day of the event.

20 Helpers have to bring their own food to eat on race day.

The Lindsay Kids of Steel Triathlon – Ontario, Canada

What is a Kids of Steel triathlon?

Triathlon is a sport that combines swimming, cycling and running. Kids of Steel events are designed to offer those aged 6 to 19 an opportunity to take part in a triathlon. It's all about having fun while keeping fit. While the races are challenging, they are short enough to make sure that everyone finishes in good time.

Who can take part?

The Lindsay triathlon is one of many such events that take place annually across the state of Ontario. These events are organised by the Ontario Association of Triathletes (OAT) and all the participants must be members of OAT. Membership costs $25 per year (for those aged 15 and under) and those without a full year-membership are required to buy a $6 one-day membership on race day in order to take part.

Distances

The Kids of Steel distances change according to the age of the athletes. For example, 14–15-year-olds will swim 500m, cycle 16km and run 5km while the 6–7 year olds will swim 50m, cycle 1.5km and run 500m. Anyone who feels unable to do a whole race on their own is welcome to enter with up to two friends. In this way each person can do at least one part of the triathlon.

What must I do to take part?

The Lindsay triathlon will take place on Sunday 21st June, starting at the Lindsay Sports Centre. On Saturday 20th you will need to check that you have registered to race and also pick up your race bag, containing your competitor number, at Lindsay Sports Centre's main reception. You will also need to get your bike and equipment checked at the Tyre Store on West Street before you can race. This must be done by a bike-repair expert and you will need to show a receipt to prove that the check was done.

If this is your first race or you just feel you need some advice from experienced triathletes and coaches, there will be a 'clinic' on June 17th at the Lindsay Sports Centre. There's no fee or registration, just come along.

Helping out

It would be impossible to run these events if we didn't have the unpaid help of so many people. If you are a parent of one of the kids taking part and you would like to get more involved on the day, then please call Andy Robinson on (708) 663-3321. He'd love to hear from you. You won't get paid, but you will get a free T-shirt and you'll be able to go to the after-race lunch party. You will also have a great time and meet lots of people.

Reading • Part 4

Questions 21 – 25

Read the text and the questions below.
For each question, mark the correct letter **A**, **B**, **C** or **D** on your answer sheet.

James Glossop – *Times* newspaper's Young Photographer of the Year

I always loved taking pictures, but the move to becoming a photographer happened when I was at university in Manchester, where I studied for my degree in English. I was asked to take pictures for a university brochure and I realised that I could make money doing something I really enjoyed.

After university, I entered *The Times* newspaper's Young Photographer of the Year competition. The prize for winning was to actually work for the paper.

Working there is great because I get a wide variety of interesting jobs. From the beginning they got me doing the big things, like political conferences and international golf tournaments. For example, I recently travelled around Greenland for 11 days for a story on climate change. I mix with the best photographers and journalists in the profession, people perhaps 20 years older than me, and I have to be at the same level as them.

I can be a serious person and that comes across in my work – which can be a bad thing if you want to make the newspaper's readers smile! When you take photos of people, they need to be able to trust you. People seem to trust me more because I work for *The Times*, and the editors there trust me, in turn, to do a good job.

In Scotland, where I'm based, I'm hoping to be on the Royal Rota, which means I'll be one of the few photographers allowed to take pictures of the Queen and her family when they visit. But, generally, I'm not interested in famous people. I like ordinary people who invite you into their home and show you their world – like the hunters and fishermen I met on my trip to Greenland.

21 What is James trying to do in this text?
    A   advise young photographers about how to get a job
    B   explain how winning a competition is helping his career
    C   describe his techniques for taking good photographs
    D   show how challenging his job at the newspaper is

22 While James was at university he discovered that
    A   he wasn't interested in studying English any more.
    B   he enjoyed taking photographs.
    C   he couldn't take the kind of photographs he wanted to.
    D   he would be able to earn money from photography.

23 What does James say about working for *The Times* newspaper?
    A   The journalists can take a long time to get a story.
    B   He prefers working on international issues.
    C   He was given main events to photograph from day one.
    D   It's difficult working with the older, more experienced professionals.

24 James believes his serious character can have an effect on
    A   the people who look at his photographs.
    B   the kind of jobs he is given.
    C   the people he takes photographs of.
    D   the way he gets on with his colleagues.

25 Which postcard might James have sent to his parents last month?

    A
    | Having a few problems – when people find out which newspaper I work for, they won't trust me to photograph them! |

    B
    | I seem to spend every day taking photos of yet another major sporting event – when will they let me do something different? |

    C
    | This is what I love doing – taking pictures of local villagers doing their daily work and letting me see what their lives are like. |

    D
    | It's been a busy week – I've been all around Scotland photographing the Prince and his wife on their tour. |

Reading Part 4

Test 3 Reading • Part 5

Questions 26 – 35

Read the text below and choose the correct word for each space.
For each question, mark the correct letter **A, B, C** or **D** on your answer sheet.

Example:

0   **A** population   **B** team   **C** crowd   **D** public

Answer: 0 A B C D (A marked)

Dolphins in Scotland

The dolphin (0) .... in the Moray Firth area of Scotland is very special. They are the most northerly bottlenose dolphins in the world with (26) .... 130 animals recorded so far.

These (27) .... dolphins are different from their relations living in warmer (28) .... such as the Indian or Pacific oceans. They are a lot bigger and fatter (4m rather than 2.5m) – this is due to the large (29) .... of fat (known as *blubber*) that their bodies (30) .... to keep them warm in the colder waters of the North Sea.

Dolphins, unlike sharks, (31) .... not automatically replace their teeth when lost – they only have one set which has to (32) .... for their whole life! They eat 8–15kg of fish a day, feeding largely on inshore (33) .... that live on the sea bed.

They live in very close family groups, (34) .... can be quite large. Local people around the Firth have seen dolphins for many years: there are reports from as (35) .... ago as 1900.

26	A	between	B	among	C	over	D	towards
27	A	proper	B	particular	C	obvious	D	usual
28	A	atmospheres	B	spaces	C	seasons	D	environments
29	A	size	B	amount	C	pile	D	load
30	A	want	B	demand	C	wish	D	need
31	A	do	B	should	C	have	D	ought
32	A	stay	B	hold	C	last	D	stop
33	A	varieties	B	sorts	C	types	D	ranges
34	A	who	B	which	C	they	D	those
35	A	much	B	enough	C	more	D	long

Test 3 Writing • Part 1

Questions 1 – 5

Here are some sentences about a novel.
For each question, complete the second sentence so that it means the same as the first.
Use no more than three words.
Write only the missing words on your answer sheet.
You may use this page for any rough work.

Example:

0   The name of the novel is *Midnight Silence*.
    The novel .... called *Midnight Silence*.

Answer: | 0 | is |

---

1   The novel was written by John Halloran.
    John Halloran .... the novel.

2   John Halloran's first book was not as good as this one.
    This book by John Halloran is much .... his first one.

3   The novel is full of interesting characters.
    There are a .... of interesting characters in the novel.

4   I have not read such a good book for a long time.
    It's a long time .... I read such a good book.

5   I'm looking forward to John Halloran's next novel.
    I .... wait until John Halloran publishes his next novel.

Test 3 — Writing • Part 2

Question 6

Your Australian friend, Alex, has sent you a photo of himself and his family.
Write an email to Alex. In your email you should:

- thank Alex for the photo
- explain why you like the photo
- say what you are going to send to Alex.

Write **35–45 words** on your answer sheet.

Test 3 — Writing • Part 3

Write an answer to **one** of the questions (**7** or **8**) in this part.
Write your answer in about **100 words** on your answer sheet.
Mark the question number in the box at the top of your answer sheet.

Question 7

- This is part of a letter you receive from an English friend.

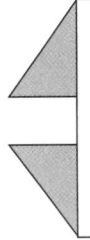

> I play the guitar – it's great fun because I love music. What music do you like to play or listen to? Do you have a favourite band or singer? Who are they and why do you like them?

- Now write a letter answering your friend's questions.
- Write your **letter** on your answer sheet.

Question 8

- Your English teacher wants you to write a story.
- This is the title for your story.

    The day I woke up late.

- Write your **story** on your answer sheet.

Test 3 Listening • Part 1

Questions 1 – 7

There are seven questions in this part.
For each question, choose the correct answer (**A**, **B** or **C**).

Example: What did the boy forget to bring home from school?

A 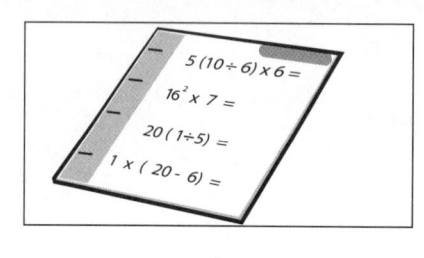   B 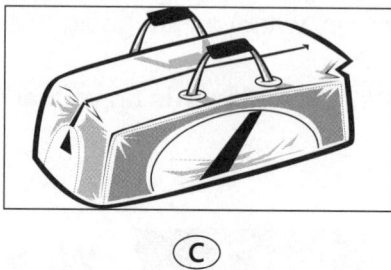   C

1   What did the girl buy for her friend's birthday?

A    B    C

2   When will the science fiction film start?

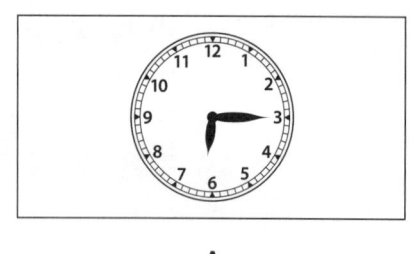

A 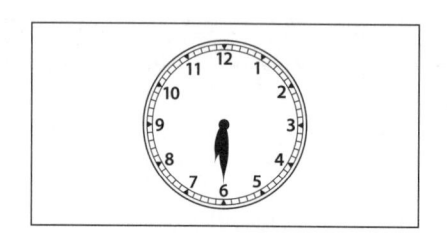   B 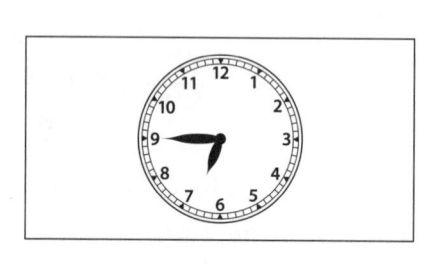   C

3   Which poster will the boy hang on his bedroom wall?

A    B    C

4 How did the girl travel to school this morning?

A  B  C

5 What will happen first in the school show?

A  B  C

6 Which book has the boy read recently?

A  B  C

7 Where is the girl's new T-shirt?

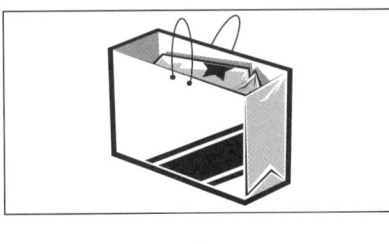

A  B 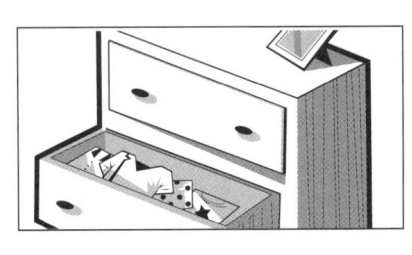 C

Test 3   Listening • Part 2

03 Questions 8 – 13

You will hear part of an interview with a boy called Simon who is helping to protect the environment. For each question, choose the correct answer **A**, **B** or **C**.

8   Simon enjoys taking his boat onto the River Stanton because
    A he knows many people who go there.
    B the speed of the water makes it exciting.
    C it is the closest river to his home town.

9   Simon noticed that the river water
    A was getting lower and lower.
    B was too dark to let him see the bottom.
    C was having a negative effect on him.

10   Simon learned more about the problem with the river
    A by looking on the internet.
    B by asking the people who owned the river.
    C by talking to his school teachers.

11   Why did Simon do a special course?
    A to join an organisation that protects the river
    B to learn about the geography of the river
    C to be able to check the water quality of the river

12   Simon is pleased because
    A the company causing the problem closed.
    B he found a way to reduce the problem.
    C he discovered new plants that live in the river.

13   Why did Simon enter the science competition?
    A to try to involve more people in helping the environment
    B to win money to help protect the river
    C to get a good grade for his school project

Test 3 — Listening • Part 3

Questions 14 – 19

You will hear some information about a café for young people.
For each question, fill in the missing information in the numbered space.

Notes about the Rainbow café

This is a special café for teenagers which opened last month.

The café is run by a **(14)** .... of ten local teenagers.

The teenagers got a grant worth **(15)** £.. to start the café.

They need some more teenagers to work as **(16)** .... in the café.

The café is currently open every **(17)** ...., from 1.30 p.m. to 6.00 p.m.

The café serves a range of hot and cold drinks and some **(18)** ....

To get more information, call **(19)** .... or visit www.youthcafe.com.

Test 3 Listening • Part 4

🎧 05 Questions 20 – 25

Look at the six sentences for this part.
You will hear a conversation between a girl, Bernice, and a boy, Jude, who study at different schools.
Decide if each sentence is correct or incorrect.
If it is correct, choose the letter **A** for **YES**. If it is not correct, choose the letter **B** for **NO**.

		YES	NO
20	Jude enjoys his usual journey to and from school.	A	B
21	Bernice has always wanted to go to Stonebridge High School.	A	B
22	Bernice thinks that her school offers students a wider range of subjects.	A	B
23	A sports team at Jude's school almost lost a game recently.	A	B
24	Bernice thinks the sports facilities at her school are excellent.	A	B
25	Bernice and Jude agree that school uniforms are a good idea.	A	B

Test 3 Speaking

Part 1

Phase 1

(possible examiner questions)

Good morning / afternoon / evening. I'm ...
What's your name?
What's your surname?
How do you spell it?
Where do you live?
Do you study English at school?
Do you like it?

Phase 2

(possible examiner questions)

What kind of clothes do you like to wear?
Which sports do you enjoy playing or watching?
Tell us what you will use English for in the future.
Tell us about a good friend of yours.

Part 2

(2–3 minutes)

I'm going to describe a situation to you.

Your English teacher has asked everyone in your class to write a **story** in English and is going to **give a prize** to the student who writes the best story. Talk together about the different things the teacher could **give** as a prize and decide **which would be the best**.

Here is a picture with some ideas to help you.

See page C3 for a picture on the topic of a **Class prize**.

Part 3

(3 minutes)

Now I'd like each of you to talk on your own about something. I'm going to give each of you a photograph of people **spending money**.

(Candidate A): Please tell us what you can see in your photograph, you have about one minute for this. (See page C9.)

(Candidate B): Your photograph also shows people **spending money**. Please tell us what you can see in your photograph, you have about one minute for this. (See page C10.)

Part 4

(3 minutes)

Your photographs showed people spending money. Now I'd like you to talk together about the different things **you** like to spend money on and **who** helps you decide what to buy.

Back-up prompts

What do you like to spend your money on?
Who helps you choose what to spend money on?
Do you enjoy shopping? Why (not)?
Where do you go to spend money?

Test 4 Reading • Part 1

Questions 1 – 5

Look at the text in each question.
What does it say?
Mark the correct letter **A**, **B** or **C** on your answer sheet.

Example:

0

> Class 8T – History lesson
>
> Miss Wade asks you to read pages 25–30 of your textbook and do task on 'transport' for homework – to hand in next Monday – as she's ill today.

A Miss Wade wants Class 8T to help her arrange transport for next Monday.

B Class 8T have work to get on with while their teacher is absent.

C Anyone in Class 8T who is ill today can hand in their homework next week.

Answer: 0 A **B** C

1

> Class 5f, go to library for today's lesson.
> Take your notes so you can revise.
> Mrs Peters

The teacher would like the students

A to look at their notes in Room 5f.

B to prepare in the library for a future test.

C to learn how to use the library properly today.

2

> Selina,
> Lotta called. I told her you were playing tennis till 3 p.m.
> She asked if you wanted to go the cinema.
> She'll call you again later.
> Mum

A Lotta wanted to know if Selina was playing tennis this afternoon.

B Lotta phoned to tell Selina that the movie starts at 3 p.m.

C Lotta wanted to invite Selina to see a film with her.

3

For Sale
Boy's racing bike
Like new, £69
Interested?
See Gavin – class 68K
Or call – 07738 599385

A Gavin, in class 68K, has a new bike for sale.

B Gavin is interested in buying a racing bike for under £70.

C Gavin is the person to contact if you want to buy a used bike.

4

Visitors to Kingsway Campsite

Please note:

No fires!

No music permitted after 9 p.m.

A Campers are allowed to listen to the radio in the early evening only.

B People staying at the campsite can have fires burning until 9 p.m.

C Only those staying at Kingsway Campsite may play music at night.

5

Findon Swimming Club

Practice: Monday 7.30 a.m.

We cannot admit any member who is not punctual

A Findon Swimming Club wants all new members to come to a practice session on Monday.

B Any members of Findon Swimming Club who arrive late will not be let into the practice session.

C The swimming club cannot confirm whether there will be a practice session on Monday.

Test 4 — Reading • Part 2

Questions 6 – 10

The teenagers below all want a book to read.
On the opposite page there are descriptions of eight books.
Decide which book would be the most suitable for the following teenagers.
For questions **6–10**, mark the correct letter (**A–H**) on your answer sheet.

6 Billy enjoys reading science fiction. He'd like to read a book that has lots of interesting pictures in it as well as an exciting story.

7 Ruby loves novels about real historical characters. She'd prefer to read a book with a film based on it so she can watch that too.

8 Max has read lots of action books and he's looking for another one but by a new writer. He'd like the main characters to be teenagers, like him.

9 Jess loves reading books that are part of a series, involving the same characters. She likes stories about relationships, and prefers those with animals in them too.

10 Cameron and his brother want to read facts about how normal people lived in the past; how they travelled, what they ate and the things they wore, etc. They'd prefer a book with drawings and diagrams.

Eight Good Books for Young Teenagers

A The History of Everything

This is a great book for young people who enjoy facts and scientific information. Most of the book is about scientific discovery through the ages – for example, how we have developed from travelling everywhere by foot or horse to the invention of the motor car. It even goes on to discuss how we might travel in the future, as we explore other planets.

B Stay True – Riding Out

Will Tabitha, Sasha and Mona manage to stay friends while performing in the horse-jumping competition against each other? Remember, they have been in worse situations. Grace Terry published her first *Stay True* novel eight years ago, but the adventures of these three friends and their horses are still as popular with readers today, in this eleventh story, as they were in the first.

C Count Down

This is Matthew Park's first novel and it's brilliant! Tom Flint is like any other 14-year-old boy until the day his scientist parents are taken by a criminal gang. In a thrilling race against time, Tom climbs mountains, dives to the bottom of the ocean and might even have to go to the moon to save them!

D Outer Limits

The action never stops in this fast-paced book with fantastic comic-strip-style drawings that teenagers will love. Follow Troy's journey to the edge of the solar system, to the last planet, where no one has visited in the past and where everyone's future may be destroyed if Troy cannot solve the mystery in time.

E Get Started

Have you ever read a science fiction short story and wished you could write one too? Then this is the book for you. Each chapter gives help and advice to new writers and encourages teenagers to pick up their pen and start being creative. This book is part of a series that helps young people develop their talents and includes books on drawing and film-making.

F Life On Screen

Ever wondered what it's like being a film star? Brad de Walt was a star from the age of 10 and is still only 18 yet he's been in many movies, from historical romances to action adventures. Brad travels the world to film but says he is only truly happy when at home with his collection of pet animals, including a monkey.

G In Action

Want to know what the inside of a working castle looked like or how long it took to ride by horse across the county? The detailed information along with the realistic pictures in this book tells you all about everyday life in the 15th century. It contains instructions for making clothes and even recipes from that period for you to try at home!

H A Short Season

There are the facts about Lady Jane Grey – an unfortunate young woman who died at the age of 16 after being Queen for just nine days – but what about the teenager who was persuaded to take the crown? In her first book, Harriet Wolfe successfully imagines the conversations, thoughts and feelings of Lady Jane, bringing the 16th century to life. And fans of the book will be pleased to know that John Grossman has just made a film of it.

Test 4 — Reading • Part 3

Questions 11 – 20

Look at the sentences below about some young people who write for a TV show.
Read the text on the opposite page to decide if each sentence is correct or incorrect.
If it is correct, mark **A** on your answer sheet.
If it is not correct, mark **B** on your answer sheet.

11 Dan wrote for the first series of the TV programme, *Catch*.

12 Dan is also one of the actors in *Catch*.

13 Dan asks his friends if he can use the actual things they say in his writing.

14 *Catch* is about a group of teenagers at a real college.

15 Each week *Catch* follows the story of one particular character.

16 The original idea for *Catch* came from the television production company.

17 Ken Thomas looked for young people to write *Catch* at various places around London.

18 Lizzie Wise was a big fan of *Catch* before she started writing for it.

19 Lizzie's background is in theatre rather than television.

20 Lizzie says the most difficult scenes to write are those where the characters say very little.

Teen writers on TV hit *Catch*

Dan Finelli is a normal teenager from north London; he goes to school, enjoys hanging out with his mates and only occasionally misses his classes. But Dan also happens to be a writer for the popular teen drama, *Catch*. The second series starts this week and the one-hour episode that Dan wrote, his very first for the show, will be on screen later in the year. This will make him one of the youngest writers of a peak-time drama ever.

'What's great about *Catch* is that the characters are exactly like the people around you,' says Dan, who also plays the part of Computer Chris in the show. 'When I'm at school and one of my friends says something funny I write it down in my notebook and use it later in the script. I never tell them I'm doing it. I just want it to sound as real as possible,' Dan adds.

Catch is about the lives of a group of 16–18-year-olds in a sixth-form college. The school doesn't really exist, but the whole show does feel very true to life. There's an episode every week and each one concentrates on an individual member of the group and tells his or her story.

The idea for the programme came from an unusual source, a father-and-son pair of writers, Ken Thomas and his son, Callum. They took their idea to a TV company and were very surprised when the company said they were keen to make it. Now, Ken and Callum are central members of the writing team but in order to build that team, Ken had to go to theatre companies and writing groups all over London to find both writers and teens to advise on the stories.

One writer he approached to join the team for the second series was Lizzie Wise. She had never heard of *Catch* when Ken first invited her to write. But Ken thought she would be right for the show because he'd read one of her plays and thought she was a very strong writer. Lizzie is only nineteen but has lots of valuable theatre experience. She says, 'I've watched much more TV than I've ever watched plays, so it wasn't difficult for me to change to TV writing. What's most challenging on *Catch* is the number of scenes in which there's hardly any talking and where the story's told through the looks the characters give each other and their body language only. These scenes take a long time to get right but they look great on the screen.'

Test 4   Reading • Part 4

Questions 21 – 25

Read the text and the questions below.
For each question, mark the correct letter **A**, **B**, **C** or **D** on your answer sheet.

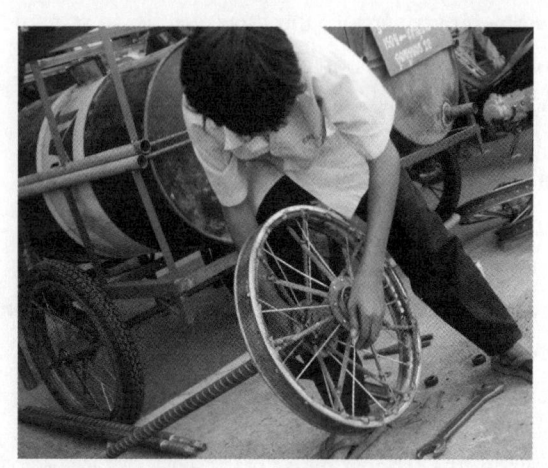

The Car

Let me tell you about a young boy who made a model car all on his own. The boy is me, six years ago when I was just 11 and the car was small and simple but in my imagination it was a high-speed, Formula 1 racing car, speeding along the race track.

It was during the school summer holidays and workmen were building a new drive and garage beside our house. While watching the workmen I had an idea. I'd build a car to drive into the garage in celebration of the new addition to our home. I told my mother and drew up complicated plans but I couldn't find the right materials, so I gave up and spent a miserable couple of days doing nothing. My mother noticed that I'd stopped working and asked me why. I explained and she suggested that maybe I should change my plans to fit the materials I did have, rather than give up.

And that's just what I did. I found small pieces of wood in my father's workshop and made my car from anything that was lying around the house. When I found a small engine from an old model plane of mine I added that. The power came from a battery attached with some wire I found in a cupboard.

By the time the garage was finished, so was my car. I called my family together outside the house, connected the wires, started the engine and placed the car on the driveway. It was fast and I had to run to the garage to rescue it before it crashed into the new door. My family began to clap and I smiled proudly. Thanks to my mother I learned the value of seeing a project through to its end. Soon I was making plans for my next project: a helicopter!

21 What is the writer trying to do in this text?
- A suggest that everybody should try making something
- B recommend a type of car that is easy to make
- C explain how he learned not to give up on an idea
- D give information about where to find good model cars

22 Why did the writer start building the car?
- A to show the workmen that he could build something too
- B to pass the time during the school holidays
- C to give to his mother as a special present
- D to celebrate the family's new garage

23 How did the writer feel about the first car he planned?
- A sad that he was unable to find suitable things to build the car with
- B annoyed that his father wouldn't let him borrow any materials
- C frustrated by how much time he'd wasted on the project
- D embarrassed by the poor quality of the car plan he drew

24 What do we find out about the car the writer finally made?
- A It was completed shortly after the garage was built.
- B It was powered by an old electric motor.
- C It went up the driveway too quickly and hit the garage.
- D Its design needed some improvements.

25 What advice might the writer give about making something?

A Always try to keep to your plans rather than change them halfway through your project.	**B** When you start a project you need as much help as you can get, so ask your friends and family to get involved.
C Look carefully around you to see what's available and what things you can reuse for your project.	**D** Don't make a car for your first project – they're difficult to get right and may not work.

Test 4 Reading • Part 5

Questions 26 – 35

Read the text below and choose the correct word for each space.
For each question, mark the correct letter **A**, **B**, **C** or **D** on your answer sheet.

Example:

0   **A** completed   **B** reached   **C** closed   **D** covered

Answer: | 0 | **A** ■ | **B** ☐ | **C** ☐ | **D** ☐ |

Kitesurfer Makes Channel Crossing

Andy Ward, a kitesurfer from Dorset in the UK, has recently **(0)** .... what is thought to be the first crossing from the Channel Islands to the coast of England.

The 70-mile journey **(26)** .... almost six hours but a delighted Mr Ward **(27)** .... that he thought it was 'all over' on a few **(28)** ....

He says, 'There were difficulties from the start. First I couldn't leave the beach **(29)** .... the wind wasn't strong enough. When I **(30)** .... finally get off the beach I worked hard but only managed to travel three or four miles in **(31)** .... first hour. Then the kite fell into the water and it was **(32)** .... before I could get it up into the air again.'

Andy has been kitesurfing for **(33)** .... three years. During the crossing, he was accompanied **(34)** .... a support boat and had a land-based team following his **(35)** .... to the English coast.

26	A	used	B	took	C	spent	D	needed
27	A	told	B	blamed	C	spoke	D	admitted
28	A	minutes	B	occasions	C	moments	D	periods
29	A	although	B	unless	C	because	D	though
30	A	was	B	had	C	will	D	did
31	A	that	B	those	C	this	D	these
32	A	times	B	lots	C	ages	D	loads
33	A	even	B	only	C	always	D	ever
34	A	by	B	with	C	at	D	beside
35	A	travel	B	movement	C	departure	D	progress

Test 4 Writing • Part 1

Questions 1 – 5

Here are some sentences about friends.
For each question, complete the second sentence so that it means the same as the first.
Use no more than three words.
Write only the missing words on your answer sheet.
You may use this page for any rough work.

Example:

0   My best friend is called Grace.
    My best friend's .... is Grace.

Answer: | 0 | name |

1   Grace and I go to Littlebrook Girls' School.
    Grace goes to Littlebrook Girls' School and .... I.

2   I'm older than Grace but I'm shorter than her.
    Although Grace isn't as .... me, she's taller than I am.

3   Grace suggested that we walk to school together every day.
    Grace said, '.................................. we walk to school together every day?'

4   Grace joined my class two years ago.
    Grace and I have been in the same class .... two years.

5   Grace's parents invited me to go on holiday with them.
    I .... to go on holiday with Grace and her family.

Test 4 — Writing • Part 2

Question 6

Your British friend, Jo, has asked you to go rock climbing this weekend.
Write an email to Jo. In your email, you should:

- refuse Jo's invitation
- explain why you can't go
- suggest something else to do together.

Write **35–45 words** on your answer sheet.

Test 4 — Writing • Part 3

Write an answer to **one** of the questions (**7** or **8**) in this part.
Write your answer in about **100 words** on your answer sheet.
Mark the question number in the box at the top of your answer sheet.

Question 7

- This is part of a letter you receive from your American friend, Charlie.

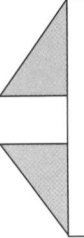

> I watched my older sister take part in a singing competition last week – she won and it was really cool! Tell me about a competition you have entered. What kind of competition would you not like to enter and why?

- Now write a letter answering your friend's questions.
- Write your **letter** on your answer sheet.

Question 8

- Your English teacher wants you to write a story.
- Your story must begin with this sentence.

    The bus stopped and I quickly jumped on it.

- Write your **story** on your answer sheet.

Test 4 — Listening • Part 1

Questions 1 – 7

There are seven questions in this part.
For each question, choose the correct answer (**A**, **B** or **C**).

Example: What did the boy forget to bring home from school?

A 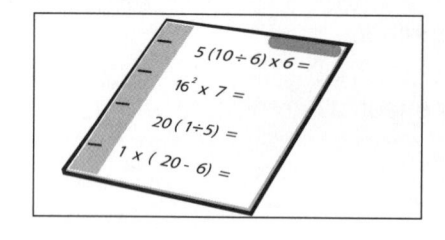   B    C (circled)

1 Who does the girl need to phone?

A    B    C

2 What was the weather like for the picnic?

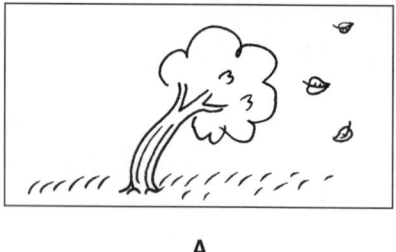

A    B    C

3 What will the boy buy from the newsagent's later this week?

A    B    C

124 | Test 4   Listening Part 1

4 How will the friends get to the party?

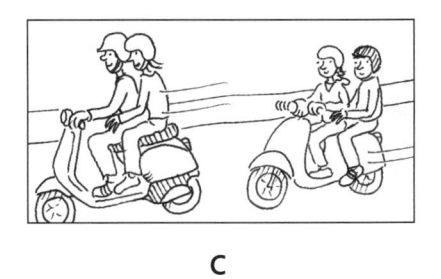

A   B   C

5 What can't the girl find?

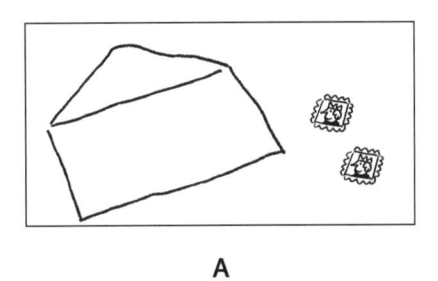

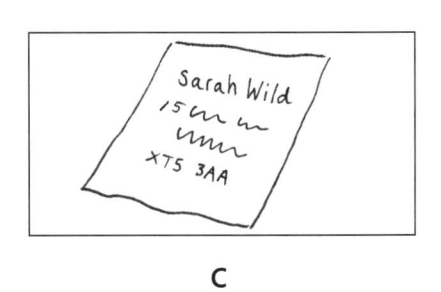

A   B   C

6 What time does the boy's bus leave?

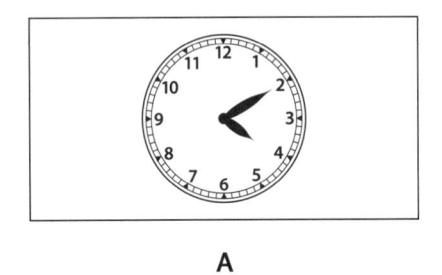

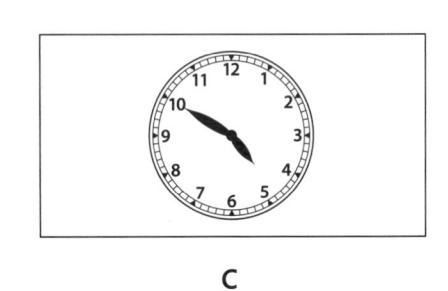

A   B   C

7 What did the girl spend her birthday money on?

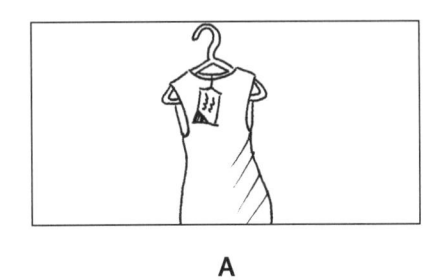

A   B   C

Listening Part 1

Test 4 — Listening • Part 2

07 Questions 8 – 13

You will hear part of an interview with a girl called Elena, a young film-maker who wrote, directed and starred in her own film. For each question, choose the correct answer **A**, **B** or **C**.

8 What does Elena say about the character she played in her film?
  A She has a very similar personality to Elena's.
  B She worries too much about people.
  C She is easily hurt by other people's actions.

9 What message does Elena want her film to communicate?
  A Value your background.
  B Believe in your own abilities.
  C Be realistic about the choices you make.

10 While filming the atmosphere was
  A difficult because it was hard to get people to work.
  B sad because of the subject matter of the film.
  C close because the difficulty of the work brought them together.

11 What does Elena say about filming?
  A The days tended to start and end at the same time.
  B They had to work every day of the week to get the film finished.
  C She filmed a similar number of scenes each day.

12 What did Elena find most challenging about making the film?
  A controlling large groups of actors when filming
  B telling people what she wanted them to do
  C having so many different jobs to do herself

13 How does Elena feel about being known as a 'teen' film-maker?
  A proud to be one of the few young film-makers working today
  B annoyed that people concentrate on her age more than her work
  C worried that she will always be thought of as a 'teen' film-maker

Test 4 — Listening • Part 3

🎧 08 Questions 14 – 19

You will hear some information about a special science lesson.
For each question, fill in the missing information in the numbered space.

Special Science Lesson

This school will speak to an astronaut working on the International Space Station!

The lesson:

7th August at 9.20 a.m.

for the whole school

will take place in the (14) ....

all questions and answers sent and received by (15) ....

The astronaut:

name: Harry Burton

length of time on Space Station: (16) ....

work Harry is doing: (17) .... on sleep while living in space

The Space Station:

travels at (18) .... miles per hour

takes 90 minutes to go round the (19) ....

Test 4 Listening • Part 4

09) Questions 20 – 25

Look at the six sentences for this part.
You will hear a conversation between a boy, Tom, and a girl, Sophie, about a TV quiz show.
Decide if each sentence is correct or incorrect.
If it is correct, choose the letter **A** for **YES**. If it is not correct, choose the letter **B** for **NO**.

		YES	NO
20	Tom and Sophie agree that the presenter of the quiz show is very funny.	A	B
21	Tom is keen on a number of programmes shown on Channel 5.	A	B
22	Tom has previously recommended this quiz show to a number of friends.	A	B
23	Tom warns that the questions become more difficult throughout the quiz.	A	B
24	Sophie is worried about being able to answer any of the questions.	A	B
25	Tom and Sophie decide to organise a school quiz together.	A	B

Test 4 — Speaking

Part 1

Phase 1
(possible examiner questions)
Good morning / afternoon / evening. I'm …
What's your name?
What's your surname?
How do you spell it?
Where do you live?
Do you study English at school?
Do you like it?

Phase 2
(possible examiner questions)
Will you use English in the future?
What did you do yesterday evening?
Tell us about a country you would like to visit.
Tell us about a film you have enjoyed watching.

Part 2

(2–3 minutes)

I'm going to describe a situation to you.

The members of a Music Club, where young people meet to talk about and listen to music, would like to have **T-shirts for all the members**. Talk together about the different designs they **can put** on the club T-shirt and decide **which would be the best**.

Here is a picture with some ideas to help you.

See page C4 for a picture on the topic of a **T-shirt design**.

Part 3

(3 minutes)

Now I'd like each of you to talk on your own about something. I'm going to give each of you a photograph of people **enjoying time outdoors**.

(Candidate A): Please tell us what you can see in your photograph, you have about one minute for this. (See page C9.)

(Candidate B): Your photograph also shows people **enjoying time outdoors**. Please tell us what you can see in your photograph, you have about one minute for this. (See page C10.)

Part 4

(3 minutes)

Your photographs showed people enjoying time outdoors. Now I'd like you to talk together about the different things **you** like doing outdoors and whether you prefer to do these things **alone** or **with friends**.

Back-up prompts
What do you like to do outdoors?
Do you prefer to do these things alone or with friends?
Where do you like to go with friends at the weekends?
What do you like doing indoors in your free time?

Test 5 — Reading • Part 1

Questions 1 – 5

Look at the text in each question.
What does it say?
Mark the correct letter **A**, **B** or **C** on your answer sheet.

Example:

0

> Class 8T – History lesson
>
> Miss Wade asks you to read pages 25–30 of your textbook and do task on 'transport' for homework – to hand in next Monday – as she's ill today.

A   Miss Wade wants Class 8T to help her arrange transport for next Monday.

B   Class 8T have work to get on with while their teacher is absent.

C   Anyone in Class 8T who is ill today can hand in their homework next week.

Answer: 0 A **B** C

1

> Hi Pete,
> Don't go to the skate park this evening. Come to my house to watch the Hilton City football match instead. It starts at 6.
> Guy

Why is Guy texting Pete?

A   to invite Pete to go to a match at the football stadium

B   to remind Pete to be at the park at 6 this evening

C   to suggest Pete watches a football game with him

2

> Where shall we go for next term's school trip?
>
> Leave your suggestions in the box at reception.

Students should

A   tell the receptionist where they want to go next term.

B   hand in their ideas for a place to visit next term.

C   leave their name at reception if they want to go on next term's trip.

3

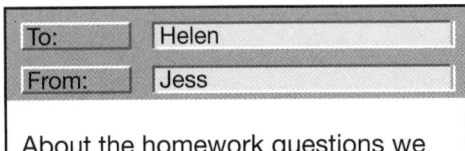

To: Helen
From: Jess

About the homework questions we have to answer together – I think Mr Gates has made a mistake. We should do the task on page 38, not page 35.

A Jess believes the teacher has given her and Helen the wrong homework.

B Jess thinks she has made a mistake answering the questions on page 38.

C Jess wonders whether Helen would like to do the homework with her.

4

Students are not permitted to use mobile phones in the library.
Please turn them off before you enter.

A Students have to leave their mobiles in a box at the library entrance.

B Students are not allowed to take any mobile phones into the library.

C Students are forbidden from speaking or texting on their phones in the library.

5

Mum
Can you remember to record my favourite programme, *Capitol High*, for me at 7? It's on Channel 5 and it's the last in the series!
Reuben

A Reuben is reminding his mum not to miss her favourite TV programme.

B Reuben is asking his mum to make a recording of his favourite show.

C Reuben is hoping to watch the last *Capitol High* at 7 p.m. with his mum.

Test 5 Reading • Part 2

Questions 6 – 10

The teenagers below all want to see a film at their school film club.
On the opposite page there are descriptions of eight films showing at the club.
Decide which film would be the most suitable for the following teenagers.
For questions **6–10**, mark the correct letter (**A–H**) on your answer sheet.

6. Hannah wants to see a romantic comedy with famous actors playing the main parts. She enjoys watching movies by new directors who use music in their films.

7. Federico only watches science fiction films. He likes movies with lots of action and special effects but he's not bothered whether the actors are famous or not.

8. Lily likes to see films that are based on novels so that she can read them too. She wants to see a recent, historical drama with a happy ending.

9. Josh wants to watch a complicated thriller with fast and funny dialogue between the characters, where you are never sure who is who until the end.

10. Chloe wants to see an old, black and white musical. She loves films involving people her own age, which include magic and are set in different worlds.

Eight Films Showing at the Film Club

A LAND

If you enjoy the romance of the high seas, this film is for you. Teenager Tom Dudley hides on a ship sailing to the Americas. He hopes to become rich but that's not how things end for Tom. Although made in the 1970s with none of the special effects we expect today, this film is a fine piece of story-telling.

B The Tower

This movie was in cinemas last year and it is director Blake Cole's best film. The film is very close to the original book and the main characters are played beautifully by two unknown young actors. They bring the past back to life and make you really care about them. So when they eventually marry you'll have a tear in your eye!

C Blaze

This film may not be full of Hollywood stars but it's full of high-speed chases, amazing computer graphics and fantastic music. In the year 4838, Jonas leaves the world he loves to look for work on a distant planet. However, he finds more than he expected. This film is based on the popular cartoon novel by Toshio Yoshida.

D Net Worth

Vince is a science geek who spends all his time playing computer games. So everyone is surprised when he suddenly becomes a millionaire after inventing a new game that people can play on the internet. Laugh out loud as Vince enjoys himself being the new 'Mr Popular' at school.

E Star Child

Sunny Jones, played by Bonny Wild, is a teenager who finds herself in the land of Zorn, under the spell of an evil queen. Although it's not in colour, the singing and dancing and Wild's wonderful voice bring the film to life and make it as enjoyable today as it was back in 1941, when it was made.

F DOWNLOAD

In director Guss Hall's first film, Katie's life is controlled by the tracks she's listening to on her iPod. She falls in love with Toby while she's listening to love songs but things go wrong between them when she starts listening to modern jazz! Well-known stars Hedda Gold and Jake Myers keep the laughs coming throughout the film.

G Making it

Fran is a real young pop singer who dreams of being famous in this documentary drama. The director, Bob Johansson, chose to film this movie in black and white and the final effect is wonderful. The film shows just how hard it is to make dreams come true.

H Catch

Harry Black is a spy, at least he says he is, but then he meets and falls in love with Greta who might actually be a spy. There are some amusing, high-speed conversations in this film, so listen carefully and enjoy the action. Are they spies or not? You'll only find out in the final scene.

Test 5 Reading • Part 3

Questions 11 – 20

Look at the sentences below about the Reach Out! camps.
Read the text on the opposite page to decide if each sentence is correct or incorrect.
If it is correct, mark **A** on your answer sheet.
If it is not correct, mark **B** on your answer sheet.

11 Each Reach Out! summer camp lasts for over a week.

12 Reach Out! camps are held in several countries around the world.

13 Camp members are encouraged to explore environmental and social topics.

14 The timetable is given to the camp members in advance of their stay.

15 Camp members do some activities in the fresh air immediately after breakfast.

16 Lessons in how to talk in front of a large audience are offered at the camp.

17 After lunch there is a choice of things for camp members to do.

18 On Action Day, camp members get the chance to visit local organisations on their own.

19 At this year's camps, Helen Yates will play songs by musicians from different countries.

20 Helen Yates has lots of interesting information about famous world leaders to share.

Reach Out! camps

Reach Out! is an organisation that runs week-long summer camps, designed to give young people the skills to be the leaders of the future. The camps help to create confident young people who wish to improve not only themselves, but the world around them. Varying in age from 12 to 17, young people come to attend the camps in Canada and the USA from across the world. They spend their time learning leadership skills, considering and discussing important issues such as pollution and health, and helping in the local community. They also meet many other young people who have the same interests and beliefs and they frequently make friendships that will last a lifetime.

There is no average day at the camp and changes are made to the timetable, which is handed out daily, to allow room for exciting events as they come up. However, camp members generally get up at 7.30 a.m. and, once they've eaten breakfast, start their day with some outdoor games to get them warmed up for the busy day ahead. There are classroom workshops in the morning on skills such as public speaking, then there's an hour for lunch at noon. From 1–2 p.m., camp members have the opportunity to select from various activities. In recent years these have included dancing, song writing, yoga and basketball.

During the members' time at camp, there is a day known as Action Day. This is when small groups go out with an adult group leader to work with organisations in the neighbourhood. Reach Out! arranges the day several weeks before the actual event and matches the interests and skills of the camp members with the organisations needing their help. This can involve organisations dealing with healthcare, housing, journalism or the environment, to name just a few.

Evenings are spent watching documentary films or listening to guest speakers. One of the speakers this year will be Helen Yates, who has worked on social projects around the world and who writes and sings her own songs about the social issues she is most concerned about. Helen has shared the stage with many of the world's political and religious leaders and has many interesting stories to tell young audiences about them. Helen's goal is to encourage the young people she meets to go out and make the world a better place.

Questions 21 – 25

Read the text and the questions below.
For each question, mark the correct letter **A, B, C** or **D** on your answer sheet.

Working in Fashion Design

I'm James Wilson and I'm the Head of Fashion Design at City College. I've had good jobs and bad in the fashion industry. I've worked for big companies and had my own company designing for individual customers. I first did a Fine Arts degree then moved into fashion and now I'm a teacher, so I'm well qualified to advise students when they ask me how to get started in a career in fashion. I tell them that first they need to find out if it really is the job for them.

Going to your local shopping mall is a great place to start. Find the person who organises the fashion shows that advertise the clothing stores in the mall and let them know that you're interested in helping out at the next one.

To get a wider picture of the business, speak to someone who makes and sells their own designs. They'll show you the less public side of the business. They might be busy but don't let that stop you. Find things out! How many hours do they work? How did they learn to make clothes? What's the toughest part of their job?

One of my students, Alex, works for Toki, a successful designer. Has he done the right thing by going to work for someone else rather than starting his own company? 'Working for Toki has added to what I learned at college,' Alex explained. 'It's great! Even though the hours are long I can learn from other people's mistakes. I've learned about tiny but very important points – like the fact that you can't just design what you want – you need to listen to your customers.'

21 What is the writer trying to do in this text?

- **A** recommend fashion companies to work for
- **B** suggest going to college to learn fashion design
- **C** describe how he succeeded as a fashion designer
- **D** explain how to discover if fashion design is for you

22 The writer suggests going to your local shopping mall to

- **A** find a job in a fashion store.
- **B** see what kind of fashion sells well.
- **C** ask to be involved in any fashion shows.
- **D** meet others who are interested in studying fashion.

23 Why is it useful to talk to someone who makes and sells their own clothes?

- **A** You can ask them lots of questions.
- **B** They can introduce you to designers.
- **C** They can teach you how to make clothes.
- **D** You can show them some of your own designs.

24 How does Alex feel about working for another designer?

- **A** It's difficult when you also have schoolwork to do.
- **B** It's a good way to learn the small details of fashion design.
- **C** It's a mistake not to start your own fashion company straight away.
- **D** It's fun because you don't have to do the same long hours as the designer.

25 What might the writer say about his own career?

- **A** I've enjoyed every single job I've ever had working in fashion.
- **B** The only thing I regret about my fashion career is never working for a large firm.
- **C** I think I've had a wide range of experience in the fashion industry.
- **D** My Education degree helped when I took the college job as Head of Fashion Design.

Test 5 Reading • Part 5

Questions 26 – 35

Read the text below and choose the correct word for each space.
For each question, mark the correct letter **A**, **B**, **C** or **D** on your answer sheet.

Example:

0   **A** earliest   **B** soonest   **C** closest   **D** nearest

Answer: | 0 | A B C D |

Bread

Bread is one of the oldest prepared foods, dating back to the **(0)** .... development of farming. Now we have a **(26)** .... choice of breads, all cut up and wrapped to take home from the supermarket, **(27)** .... bread has not always been so cheap or easily **(28)** ....

Breads dating back 10,000 years were flat breads that **(29)** .... not use yeast to make them rise. **(30)** .... of flat breads still eaten today are Indian chapattis and Mexican tortillas. It was in Ancient Egypt, **(31)** .... the banks of the river Nile, that the wheat used to make bread was grown in large **(32)** .... Egyptian bakers experimented to create raised breads and also invented closed ovens. Bread became **(33)** .... important and it was often used instead of money.

The Romans enjoyed eating bread, and rich people **(34)** .... to have the more expensive white breads. White bread is still to this **(35)** .... the most popular variety in Europe and North America.

26	**A** high	**B** long	**C** huge	**D** strong
27	**A** so	**B** but	**C** that	**D** while
28	**A** ready	**B** allowed	**C** possible	**D** available
29	**A** did	**B** would	**C** had	**D** must
30	**A** Methods	**B** Examples	**C** Reasons	**D** Ways
31	**A** within	**B** about	**C** inside	**D** along
32	**A** lengths	**B** weights	**C** quantities	**D** sizes
33	**A** very	**B** even	**C** much	**D** only
34	**A** said	**B** demanded	**C** suggested	**D** told
35	**A** time	**B** moment	**C** hour	**D** day

Test 5 Writing • Part 1

Questions 1 – 5

Here are some sentences about a football team.
For each question, complete the second sentence so that it means the same as the first.
Use no more than three words.
Write only the missing words on your answer sheet.
You may use this page for any rough work.

Example:

0 I play for the school football team.

   I'm one of the .... in the school football team.

Answer: | 0 | players |

---

1 Our coach, Mr Groves, said we had to practise every week.

   'You .... to practise every week,' said Mr Groves, our coach.

2 Our team is the best in the local school league.

   There isn't a .... team than ours in the local school league.

3 Last week, we were given new team shirts and shorts to wear.

   Last week, Mr Groves .... new team shirts and shorts to wear.

4 I like to play football in my free time.

   I like to spend my free time .... football.

5 'Do you want to join the football team, Harvey?' I asked.

   I asked my friend Harvey .... wanted to join the football team.

Test 5 Writing • Part 2

Question 6

You were at your British friend Sue's house yesterday and you broke Sue's alarm clock while you were there.
Write an email to Sue. In your email you should:

- apologise
- describe what happened
- offer to replace it.

Write **35–45 words** on your answer sheet.

Test 5 Writing • Part 3

Write an answer to **one** of the questions (**7** or **8**) in this part.
Write your answer in about **100 words** on your answer sheet.
Mark the question number in the box at the top of your answer sheet.

Question 7

- This is part of a letter you receive from an Australian friend.

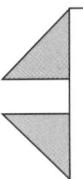

> It's summer now, so I spend nearly all my time outside with my friends. What do you do in your country when the weather is sunny? What's your favourite type of weather and why?

- Now write a letter answering your friend's questions.
- Write your **letter** on your answer sheet.

Question 8

- Your English teacher has asked you to write a story.
- This is the title for your story.

   My Great Adventure

- Write your **story** on your answer sheet.

Test 5 — Listening • Part 1

CD3 02 Questions 1 – 7

There are seven questions in this part.
For each question, choose the correct answer (**A**, **B** or **C**).

Example: What did the boy forget to bring home from school?

A 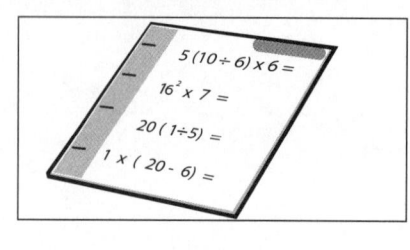   B    C

1 What is the date of the end-of-year party at school?

A 6th June
B 13th June
C 12th July

2 Which notebook did the girl buy?

A    B    C

3 Which musical instrument does the boy want to learn to play?

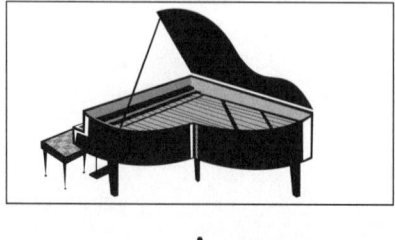

A    B 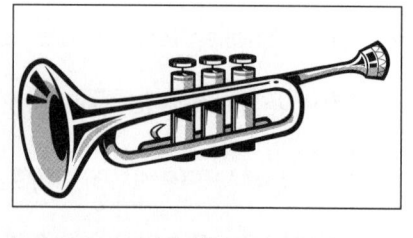   C

4 How did the girl find out about the party?

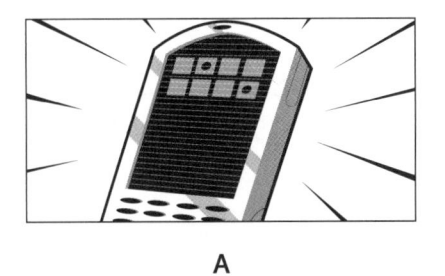

A 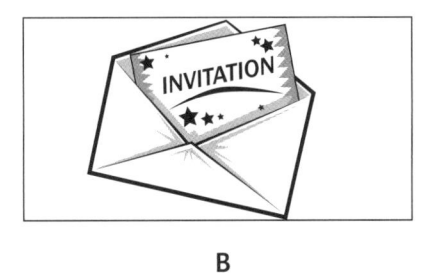   B 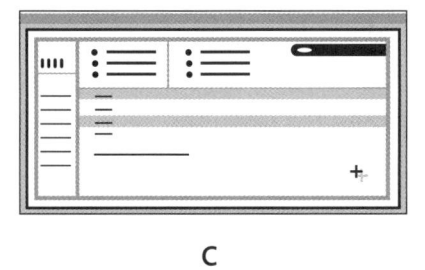   C

5 Which show do they decide to see?

A 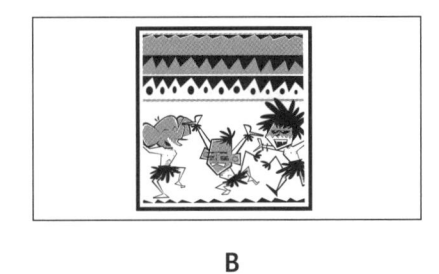   B    C

6 How did the boy get home from school yesterday?

A    B    C

7 Where is the boy's mobile phone now?

A    B 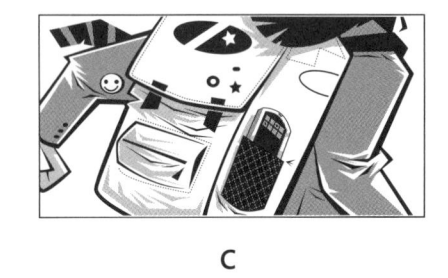   C

Test 5 Listening • Part 2

🎧 03 Questions 8 – 13

You will hear a man talking on the radio about a number of local sporting events happening over the next week. For each question, choose the correct answer **A**, **B** or **C**.

8 The cycling event on Saturday is
   A open for anyone to join in on the day.
   B only for teams of cyclists.
   C over two distances.

9 The athletics competition being held this weekend will
   A take place at a new stadium.
   B be shown on national television.
   C be a chance to see some world-class runners.

10 What is interesting about the diving competition on Sunday?
   A It is a new competition.
   B A local teenager is in it.
   C A world record might be broken.

11 What does the speaker say about the tennis tournament?
   A There are no more tickets left.
   B Ticket prices are more expensive this year.
   C Listeners can enter a competition to win tickets.

12 The speaker advises that people going to see the surfing competition
   A should wear warm clothes.
   B should go to the beach on the bus.
   C should take a picnic lunch with them.

13 The free yoga sessions on Sunday afternoon
   A are for all ages.
   B need to be booked in advance.
   C will take place in a sports centre.

Test 5 — Listening • Part 3

Questions 14 – 19

You will hear a teacher talking about some visitors coming to speak at the school. For each question, fill in the missing information in the numbered space.

Visiting Speakers

Series of talks by visiting speakers:

monthly

on first **(14)** ....

at 4.45 p.m.

The first talk – Ellie Brown

Date: 2nd November

Ellie's job: **(15)** ....

Ellie will:

talk about her education and studies

talk about her visit to **(16)** ....

play a video and show photographs

The second talk – Harry Fowler

Date: **(17)** ....

Harry's job: camera operator

Topic of talk: making **(18)** .... films.

Harry's book: *Behind the Lens*

Book costs: **(19)** £ .... at the talk

Test 5 — Listening • Part 4

🎧 05 Questions 20 – 25

Look at the six sentences for this part.
You will hear a conversation between a girl, Jill, and a boy, Guss, about an adventure park they have both visited.
Decide if each sentence is correct or incorrect.
If it is correct, choose the letter **A** for **YES**. If it is not correct, choose the letter **B** for **NO**.

		YES	NO
20	Jill's parents asked her to save up her money for the adventure park.	A	B
21	Guss's uncle wanted to go on the rides with Guss and Todd.	A	B
22	Jill and Guss agree that Thunder Mountain is the best ride in the park.	A	B
23	Jill believes the park will be busy whatever the weather is like.	A	B
24	Guss wants to revisit one particular part of the adventure park.	A	B
25	Jill and Guss both think that improvements are needed at the adventure park.	A	B

Test 5 — Speaking

Part 1

Phase 1

(possible examiner questions)

Good morning / afternoon / evening. I'm …
What's your name?
What's your surname?
How do you spell it?
Where do you live?
Do you study English at school?
Do you like it?

Phase 2

(possible examiner questions)

How did you travel to school today?
What are you going to do this weekend?
Tell us about where you would like to go on holiday. Why?
Tell us about the food you enjoy eating.

Part 2

(2–3 minutes)

I'm going to describe a situation to you.

A group of school children are going to **the city for the day**. They are going to the theatre in the afternoon but they need something to do for two hours in the morning.

Talk together about **the different things they could do in the city for two hours** and decide which would be **the best**.

Here is a picture with some ideas to help you.

See page C5 for a picture on the topic of **Two hours in the city**.

Part 3

(3 minutes)

Now I'd like each of you to talk on your own about something. I'm going to give each of you a photograph of people **reading**.

(Candidate A): Please tell us what you can see in your photograph, you have about one minute for this. (See page C11.)

(Candidate B): Your photograph also shows people reading. Please tell us what you can see in your photograph, you have about one minute for this. (See page C12.)

Part 4

(3 minutes)

Your photographs showed young people reading. Now I'd like you to talk together about the different things **you** read and say which you **enjoy** reading and which you **don't enjoy** so much.

Back-up prompts

What do you read?
What do you enjoy / not enjoy reading?
What did you like reading when you were younger?
What will you read tomorrow?

Test 6 — Reading • Part 1

Questions 1 – 5

Look at the text in each question.
What does it say?
Mark the correct letter **A**, **B** or **C** on your answer sheet.

Example:

0

> Class 8T – History lesson
>
> Miss Wade asks you to read pages 25–30 of your textbook and do task on 'transport' for homework – to hand in next Monday – as she's ill today.

A   Miss Wade wants Class 8T to help her arrange transport for next Monday.

B   Class 8T have work to get on with while their teacher is absent.

C   Anyone in Class 8T who is ill today can hand in their homework next week.

Answer: 0 A **B** C

1

> Sam
> I've just arrived at the pool and forgot that it's closed today, so don't bother coming here. I'll see you at the park entrance at 10 instead.
> Jake

Jake wants Sam to

A   arrive at the pool earlier than planned.

B   meet him at a different location.

C   remember to bring his swimming things.

2

> **Library**
>
> Replace books when you have finished
>
> Do not leave them on the desks

Library users

A   must put the books back on the shelves.

B   should take their books to the main desk.

C   cannot take any books out of this area.

3

Tania!

Katy called. She said she'll be late arriving at the party tonight but if you still want a lift with Katy and her dad then text her before 5 p.m. Mum

A Katy has invited Tania to her party tonight.

B Tania's mum wants to know how Tania is going to the party.

C Tania needs to contact Katy about getting a ride to the party.

4

New School Diaries available now!
Ask at office – 10% discount on first 100 sold.

A You can now buy last year's diary at a lower price.

B If you are one of the first to buy a diary, you'll pay less.

C There are only 100 school diaries left in the office.

5

This plastic cover protects your new phone.
Remove before use.
Be responsible – recycle waste plastics.

A You need to take the plastic cover off your phone so you can start using it.

B You should put a plastic cover over your phone to stop it getting damaged.

C You can reuse this plastic cover to protect your phone when you're not using it.

Reading Part 1

Test 6 Reading • Part 2

Questions 6 – 10

The young people below all want to play tennis during their school holiday.
On the opposite page there are descriptions of eight tennis courses.
Decide which tennis course would be the most suitable for the following young people.
For questions **6–10**, mark the correct letter (**A–H**) on your answer sheet.

6. Sunita needs help to improve her tennis skills, so wants to have individual coaching. She'd like to play tennis outdoors in the mornings and do other activities in the afternoons.

7. Paul and his brother do not know how to play tennis, so want to spend a week learning. They would prefer to be outside in a small group and will need to borrow rackets.

8. Zoe and her parents enjoy playing tennis together. They'd like to get advice from an expert and want lots of practice. They'd prefer to be near the coast.

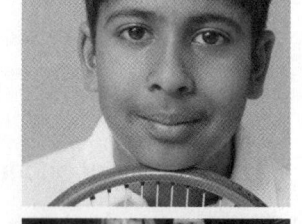

9. Ali is looking for a three-day tennis break in the countryside. He can't play tennis but he does have all the equipment. He'd like to have fun and meet other teenagers.

10. Vanessa is a good tennis player and her friends are almost as good. Their tennis course will be for a week during the winter, so they want to be able to play inside.

Tennis Courses

A Weybridge Tennis

We run two-day, weekend courses all through the summer. Our tennis centre is next to one of the most beautiful beaches in the north. You will have the chance to play tennis all day and be taught by very experienced coaches. Unfortunately, this year we are not running any courses for adults.

B Gary Dymond's Tennis Centre

We have years of experience teaching beginners tennis and provide all the equipment you'll need. Because we're situated in the busy seaside town of Rye there is always something to do when you're not playing tennis. Our tennis courses are for teenagers only and run throughout the summer, for seven days. Class sizes are kept to a maximum of six.

C Match Point

Join us on our farm where we have six outdoor courts and space for 25 guests. It's the perfect place to enjoy nature and learn a completely new sport. Young people (10 years +) are welcome to stay from two days up to a week. Everyone needs to bring their own rackets, clothes, etc. as only balls are available to buy.

D Racket and Ball

We offer tennis courses for players at all levels in one of the most interesting cities in the country. Tennis sessions run from 9 a.m. – 12.30 p.m. You can join a group or have one-to-one instruction. After lunch each day we'll take you to some wonderful places in this amazing city. Our outdoor courts have lights so you can play again in the evenings.

E Ace Tennis

Never played tennis before? Want to find out if you like it before you buy an expensive tennis racket? Why not come to our indoor tennis centre for a weekend of fun activities in the mornings and tennis games in the afternoon? Fifty places are available and all equipment is provided.

F Lifelong Tennis

Come to us for year-round tennis courses at our modern tennis school near the town centre. Our indoor courts allow us to offer tennis coaching to all levels and age groups whatever the weather. Classes are in groups of 15 and courses run from seven to ten days. Please bring your own rackets and tennis clothes.

G Top Tennis

Our summer courses are for young tennis players who are already very skilled and are thinking of playing professionally. We have a number of experts on our staff who will give advice and coaching throughout the week. This is a serious course for people who want to play from morning to night!

H Advantage Tennis Breaks

Our group courses are for all ages and are designed to help people who can already play strengthen their tennis skills. We have highly-qualified coaches on hand to give you tips and we'll even video your playing. Our 12 outdoor courts are just five minutes from Fingle beach and classes can be booked between 8.30 a.m. – 9 p.m. each day.

Test 6 — Reading • Part 3

Questions 11 – 20

Look at the sentences below about a man called Mo Park, who likes collecting things.
Read the text on the opposite page to decide if each sentence is correct or incorrect.
If it is correct, mark **A** on your answer sheet.
If it is not correct, mark **B** on your answer sheet.

11 Mo bought a film in its metal container at a local antiques shop.

12 Mo was very keen to open the parcel with the film in it.

13 Mo believed that the person who sold him the film had little idea what was inside.

14 When Mo looked at the film he recognised the person in it.

15 One of Mo's friends had the special equipment Mo needed in order to watch the film.

16 Mo had lots of problems trying to find any information about the film.

17 Mo got some information about the film from an organisation called the British Film Institute.

18 Mo stopped working so that he could concentrate on researching the film.

19 The film, *Zepped*, was made at the same time as the film *Mary Poppins*.

20 Mo is unsure about what he is going to do with the film.

Mo Park – collector

Mo Park loves collecting things. He often goes to antique sales to buy old pottery, silver and boxes. He is fascinated by old things, so when he was online one evening and saw an old metal film container for sale, he had to buy it. He was attracted by the film container because it looked so old and interesting. The price was at £3, so he typed in £3.20 and won the auction. When it was delivered by post a couple of days later he had forgotten all about it. When he did eventually open it, the container was indeed as knocked around as it had looked in the photograph. Mo was pretty sure that whoever had sold it to him didn't know anything about the film within it.

When Mo took the film out and held it up to the light he could see a familiar figure. It was the famous actor, Charlie Chaplin. About two weeks later, Mo and some friends watched the whole film. To do this Mo had to look in the phone book and find someone with a specialised machine to show it on. As they watched they all got a shock. The film was called *Zepped* but none of the audience had ever heard of it.

Mo decided to find out all he could about it. He looked online but there was nothing. He read biographies of Chaplin but there was no mention of the film. He even contacted the British Film Institute but with no success. Then he got lucky. On a research trip to the British Library's newspaper archive he discovered a reference to *Zepped*. He found a poster and an article that explained that the film was released in England in 1916. It was a short comedy shown to British soldiers during the First World War but it had disappeared after that.

A good friend of Mo's became just as interested in the film as Mo. Together they went to Hollywood and Chaplin's old film studios to find out more. To do this, Mo put other people in charge of running his company so that he could work on the film full time. What Mo discovered was that *Zepped* was one of a kind. No other film made at that time used the technique of mixing live action with cartoon animation. That did not happen until nearly sixty years later, in *Mary Poppins*. Mo has been told that the film, at just seven and a half minutes long, could be worth more than a million pounds. But then who knows? He might sell it or he might keep it. It's not the money that excites Mo; it's the fact that he found such a treasure in such an everyday place.

Test 6 Reading • Part 4

Questions 21 – 25

Read the text and the questions below.
For each question, mark the correct letter **A**, **B**, **C** or **D** on your answer sheet.

Mary-Jess Leaverland

When 19-year-old Mary-Jess Leaverland sang for 70 million TV viewers nobody back home in England knew anything about it. Her victory in the talent show, *I Want to Sing to the Stars* was seen by five times as many people as watch a similar UK show, called *The X Factor*, but they were all from the Chinese region of Jiangsu, as that's the only place the programme is shown.

Mary-Jess was in China to study the language as part of her university course when she entered the competition. A friend had invited her to watch him in a TV quiz show. On their way they passed the talent show's studios. Mary-Jess went in, found a producer and sang for him. During the competition she had classes as usual then went to the studios in the evenings. When she wasn't on stage she was busy doing her homework.

Mary-Jess used her £900 prize money to fly home to see her mum. When she returned there were no recording contracts to sign or concerts to perform in. She told her mum, who's also a good singer, how amazed she was that she was chosen as the winner, then the two of them chatted happily about their plans to start singing together again at clubs around their home town. It was only later that Mary-Jess's mum thought it might be fun to tell the local newspaper about her daughter's win. Yet, within 24 hours, Mary-Jess's story had appeared nationally and just weeks later she had a manager, a lawyer and was off to New York with record companies fighting to sign her as one of their artists. Mary-Jess's singing career had started.

21 What is the writer trying to do in this text?
- **A** encourage people to watch a particular TV music programme
- **B** suggest how to get a career as a professional singer
- **C** describe someone's life-long ambition to become world famous
- **D** explain what happened to someone after winning a competition

22 What does the text say about *I Want to Sing to the Stars*?
- **A** It's less popular than another show called *The X Factor*.
- **B** It's shown in several countries across Asia.
- **C** It's a talent competition made in China.
- **D** It's the most popular TV show in China.

23 What was Mary-Jess's reason for going to China?
- **A** She went there to be in a singing competition.
- **B** She was there learning to speak Chinese.
- **C** She was teaching at a Chinese university.
- **D** She was visiting a friend there.

24 How did Mary-Jess feel when she first returned to England?
- **A** surprised that she had won the competition
- **B** annoyed that she got so little in prize money
- **C** worried about the concerts she would have to do
- **D** amazed by all the attention from the UK newspapers

25 Which text message might Mary-Jess's mother have on her mobile phone?

- **A** Where did I get my talent from, Mum? There are no other singers in our family that I know about.
- **B** I've never sung in front of anyone in my life! Why did I ever agree to be in this competition?
- **C** I've got so much work to do for my teacher! Do you think I should take it with me to the TV studios?
- **D** A Chinese TV company has offered me my own weekly show! Should I sign the contract, Mum?

Reading Part 4

Test 6 — Reading • Part 5

Questions 26 – 35

Read the text below and choose the correct word for each space.
For each question, mark the correct letter **A**, **B**, **C** or **D** on your answer sheet.

Example:

| 0 | **A** consists | **B** forms | **C** stands | **D** holds |

Answer: 0 **A** B C D

Hot-air Balloons

A hot-air balloon **(0)** .... of three basic parts. The large balloon is **(26)** .... as the 'envelope' and is made of nylon – the same material used to produce kites, sails and sleeping bags. There are burners under the envelope to heat the air inside and finally a basket **(27)** .... the passengers stand. From this **(28)** .... the passengers can enjoy the views of the countryside below.

(29) .... understand what allows the balloon to lift into the air you must know about 'convection' or heat transfer. The scientific **(30)** .... is that by heating the air inside the envelope you increase the space the air **(31)** .... When this happens, **(32)** .... air gets pushed out of the envelope. With less air in the envelope, it **(33)** .... lighter and therefore able to travel up. Once the burner is shut off, however, the **(34)** .... thing happens. Cold air from outside enters the envelope, **(35)** .... the balloon heavier and it starts to fall.

26	A	said	B	told	C	called	D	known
27	A	which	B	that	C	where	D	when
28	A	position	B	situation	C	place	D	condition
29	A	For	B	By	C	From	D	To
30	A	reason	B	explanation	C	thought	D	purpose
31	A	needs	B	wants	C	receives	D	demands
32	A	much	B	all	C	many	D	some
33	A	changes	B	moves	C	becomes	D	develops
34	A	different	B	opposite	C	other	D	unequal
35	A	causing	B	letting	C	making	D	allowing

Test 6 — Writing • Part 1

Questions 1 – 5

Here are some sentences about a drama club.
For each question, complete the second sentence so that it means the same as the first.
Use no more than three words.
Write only the missing words on your answer sheet.
You may use this page for any rough work.

Example:

0   There is a drama club at my school.

   We .... **a drama club at my school.**

Answer: | 0 | have |

1   One of my friends asked me to go to the club with her.

   A friend of .... **asked me to go to the club with her.**

2   The drama club only starts at 4 p.m., after school finishes.

   The drama club .... **until 4 p.m., after school finishes.**

3   Learning how to act is something I really enjoy doing.

   I find it very .... **learning how to act.**

4   Last month I was asked by Miss Clark to read a new play.

   Last month Miss Clark .... **to read a new play.**

5   The play we are working on now is the longest we've ever done.

   We've never worked on .... **long play as the current one.**

Test 6 Writing • Part 2

Question 6

You are arranging a class picnic for you and your friends, including your English friend, Charlie. Write a card to Charlie. In your card you should:

- invite Charlie to the picnic
- explain why the class is having a picnic
- suggest something Charlie could bring to the picnic.

Write **35–45 words** on your answer sheet.

Test 6 Writing • Part 3

Write an answer to **one** of the questions (**7** or **8**) in this part.
Write your answer in about **100 words** on your answer sheet.
Mark the question number in the box at the top of your answer sheet.

Question 7

- This is part of a letter you receive from a Canadian friend.

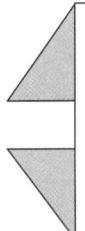

> I've just moved to a new town and don't know anyone here. What are some good ways of meeting people? Have you got any advice you can give me?

- Now write a letter answering your friend's questions.
- Write your **letter** on your answer sheet.

Question 8

- Your English teacher has asked you to write a story.
- Your story must begin with this sentence.

   I quickly started to open the large box.

- Write your **story** on your answer sheet.

Test 6 Listening • Part 1

Questions 1 – 7

There are seven questions in this part.
For each question, choose the correct answer (**A**, **B** or **C**).

Example: What did the boy forget to bring home from school?

A 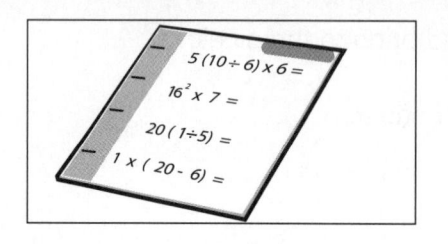   B    **C**

1   Which programme will be shown next on this TV channel?

A    B    C

2   What did the girl eat for lunch?

A    B    C

3   Where are the boy and his family going on holiday?

A    B    C

4 When will the girl be in the race?

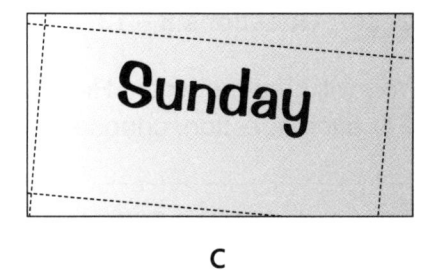

   A Wednesday   B Saturday   C Sunday

5 Which animal did the boy enjoy seeing at the zoo?

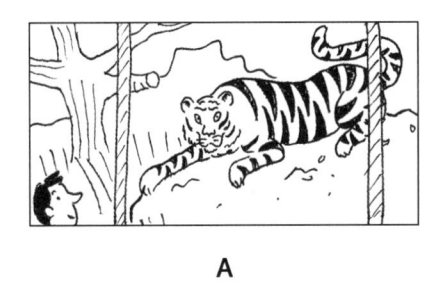

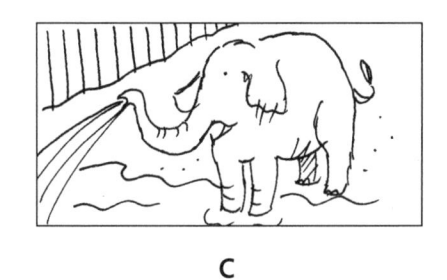

6 What has the girl just received in the post?

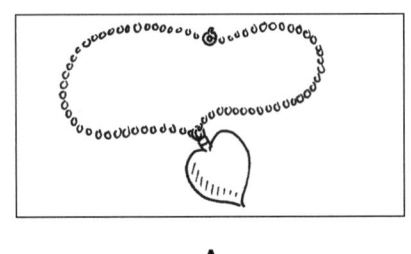

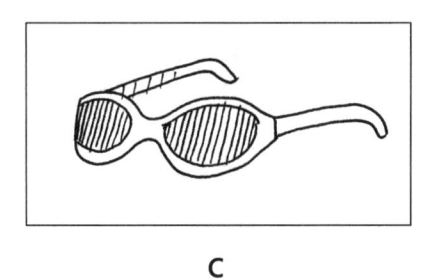

7 How did the boy find out about the cancelled lesson?

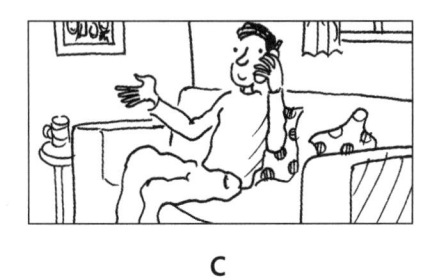

Test 6 Listening • Part 2

07 Questions 8 – 13

You will hear the writer, Holly Boland, talking about her books and her interest in nature and wildlife. For each question, choose the correct answer **A**, **B** or **C**.

8   What made Holly start writing when she was young?
   A   keeping a diary each day
   B   wanting to remember her dreams
   C   completing a homework project

9   Holly tells the story about the starfish to show
   A   how to keep wild animals at home.
   B   how to enjoy wildlife without hurting it.
   C   how to find the most interesting animals in the wild.

10   What does Holly think is the most interesting thing about nature?
   A   that animals live so close to us
   B   that there is so much to learn
   C   that nature is so beautiful

11   What does Holly say about trees?
   A   They have lots of uses.
   B   They are everywhere.
   C   They are often unnoticed.

12   Holly hopes that her young readers
   A   learn how to discover nature for themselves.
   B   improve their general reading skills.
   C   go on to study nature at college or university.

13   What kind of books does Holly enjoy reading in her spare time?
   A   classic novels
   B   cookery books
   C   field guides

Test 6 — Listening • Part 3

08 Questions 14 – 19

You will hear a recorded message about a competition.
For each question, fill in the missing information in the numbered space.

Competition

Type of competition: Painting

Date to send in paintings: **(14)** ....

Prize: Winners will have their paintings shown at the School of Arts.

Number of entries last year: **(15)** ....

Look online at www.youngpainter.org to see winning paintings from last year.

Topic for this year's competition: The **(16)** ....

Here are some ideas:

- my world – my family, my home
- inventions –travel, robots
- issues – global warming, pollution

Everyone gets a **(17)** .... to put on their wall.

School groups are welcome to enter.

Go to **www.youngpainter.org** to download:

- all entry information
- a **(18)** .... to complete and send in with the painting

Or call 01748 338294 to order an information pack.

Special workshop for schools:

with artist Barry Wells from **(19)** ...., – learn to draw cartoons

Test 6 — Listening • Part 4

09 Questions 20 – 25

Look at the six sentences for this part.
You will hear a conversation between a boy, Casper, and a girl, Rosie, about a computer game called *City Car 2*.
Decide if each sentence is correct or incorrect.
If it is correct, choose the letter **A** for **YES**. If it is not correct, choose the letter **B** for **NO**.

		YES	NO
20	Casper has had the game *City Car 2* since his birthday.	A	B
21	Casper and Rosie agree that *City Car 2* is better than *City Car 1*.	A	B
22	Rosie thinks the game is very complicated to play.	A	B
23	Casper knows where to get useful tips on how to play the game.	A	B
24	Rosie prefers to play computer games online with friends.	A	B
25	Rosie is confident that she can get a better score than Casper.	A	B

Test 6 — Speaking

Part 1

Phase 1

(possible examiner questions)

Good morning / afternoon / evening. I'm ...
What's your name?
What's your surname?
How do you spell it?
Where do you live?
Do you study English at school?
Do you like it?

Phase 2

(possible examiner questions)

What do you usually eat for breakfast?
What will you do this evening?
Tell us about what you enjoy doing with your friends or family.
Tell us about a normal day at school.

Part 2

(2–3 minutes)

I'm going to describe a situation to you.

A friend of yours is going to run in an eight-kilometre race next month and needs to **get fit quickly**. Talk together about the different things he could do to **get fit** and decide which would be **the best**.

Here is a picture with some ideas to help you.

See page C6 for a picture on the topic of **Keeping fit**.

Part 3

(3 minutes)

Now I'd like each of you to talk on your own about something. I'm going to give each of you a photograph of people **making things**.

(Candidate A): Please tell us what you can see in your photograph, you have about one minute for this. (See page C11.)

(Candidate B): Your photograph also shows people making things. Please tell us what you can see in your photograph, you have about one minute for this. (See page C12.)

Part 4

(3 minutes)

Your photographs showed young people making things. Now I'd like you to talk together about the different things **you** like to make, and say **why** you enjoy doing it and **how** you first learned to do it.

Back-up prompts

What do you make?
Why do you enjoy making it/them?
How did you learn to make this/these?
What is difficult about making this/these?

UNIVERSITY of CAMBRIDGE
ESOL Examinations

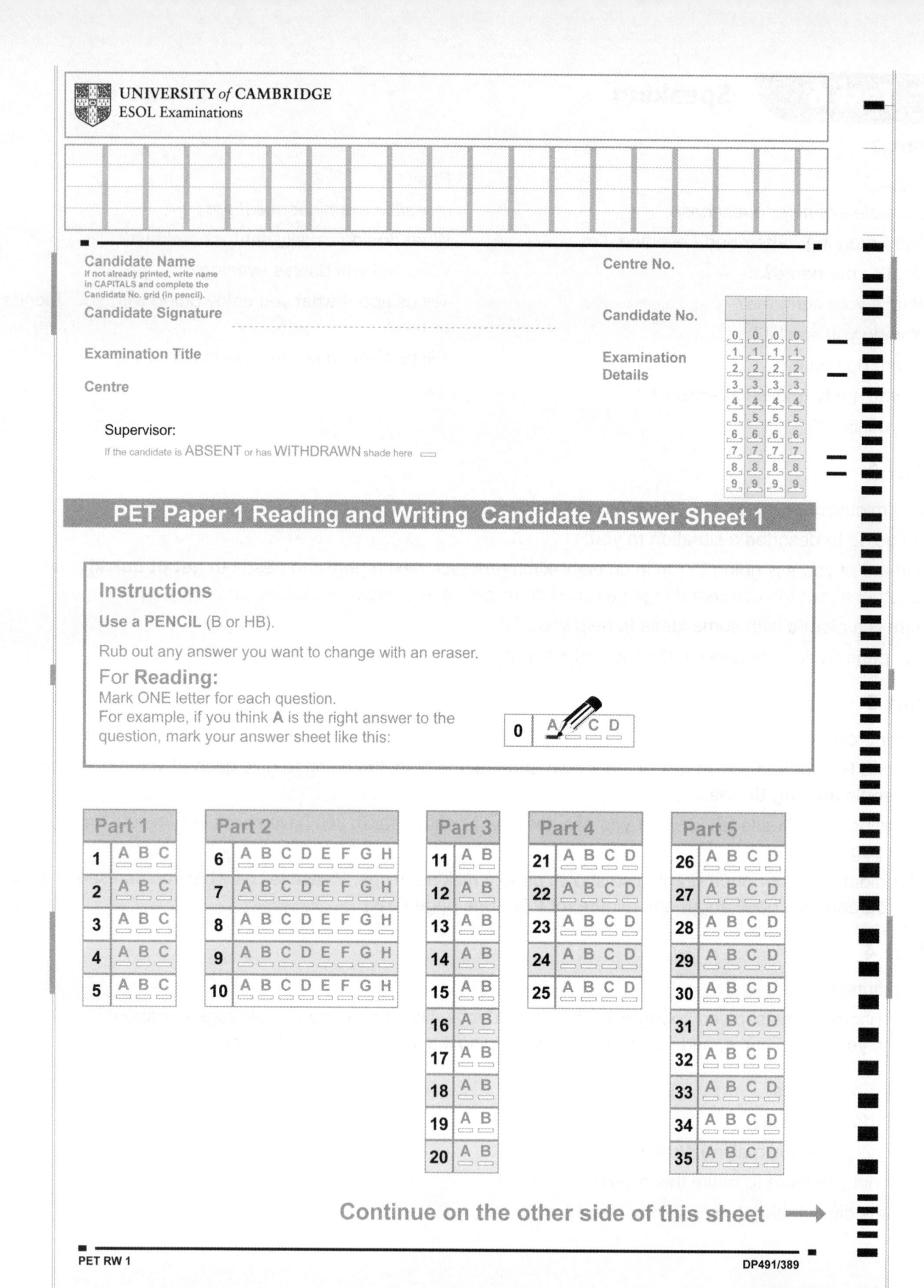

Candidate Name
If not already printed, write name in CAPITALS and complete the Candidate No. grid (in pencil).

Candidate Signature

Examination Title

Centre

Supervisor:
If the candidate is ABSENT or has WITHDRAWN shade here ▭

Centre No.

Candidate No.

Examination Details

PET Paper 1 Reading and Writing Candidate Answer Sheet 1

Instructions

Use a PENCIL (B or HB).

Rub out any answer you want to change with an eraser.

For Reading:
Mark ONE letter for each question.
For example, if you think **A** is the right answer to the question, mark your answer sheet like this:

Part 1	Part 2	Part 3	Part 4	Part 5
1 A B C	6 A B C D E F G H	11 A B	21 A B C D	26 A B C D
2 A B C	7 A B C D E F G H	12 A B	22 A B C D	27 A B C D
3 A B C	8 A B C D E F G H	13 A B	23 A B C D	28 A B C D
4 A B C	9 A B C D E F G H	14 A B	24 A B C D	29 A B C D
5 A B C	10 A B C D E F G H	15 A B	25 A B C D	30 A B C D
		16 A B		31 A B C D
		17 A B		32 A B C D
		18 A B		33 A B C D
		19 A B		34 A B C D
		20 A B		35 A B C D

Continue on the other side of this sheet ➡

PET RW 1   DP491/389

REPRODUCED WITH THE PERMISSION OF CAMBRIDGE ESOL © UCLES 2011   Photocopiable

For **Writing (Parts 1 and 2):**

Write your answers clearly in the spaces provided.

Part 1: Write your answers below.	Do not write here
1	1 1 0
2	1 2 0
3	1 3 0
4	1 4 0
5	1 5 0

Part 2 (Question 6): Write your answer below.

Put your answer to Writing Part 3 on Answer Sheet 2 →

Do not write below (Examiner use only)
0 1 2 3 4 5

REPRODUCED WITH THE PERMISSION OF CAMBRIDGE ESOL © UCLES 2011 Photocopiable

You must write within the grey lines.

Answer only one of the two questions for Part 3.
Tick the box to show which question you have answered.
Write your answer below. Do not write on the barcodes.

Part 3	Question 7	Question 8

Examiner Mark:

UNIVERSITY of CAMBRIDGE
ESOL Examinations

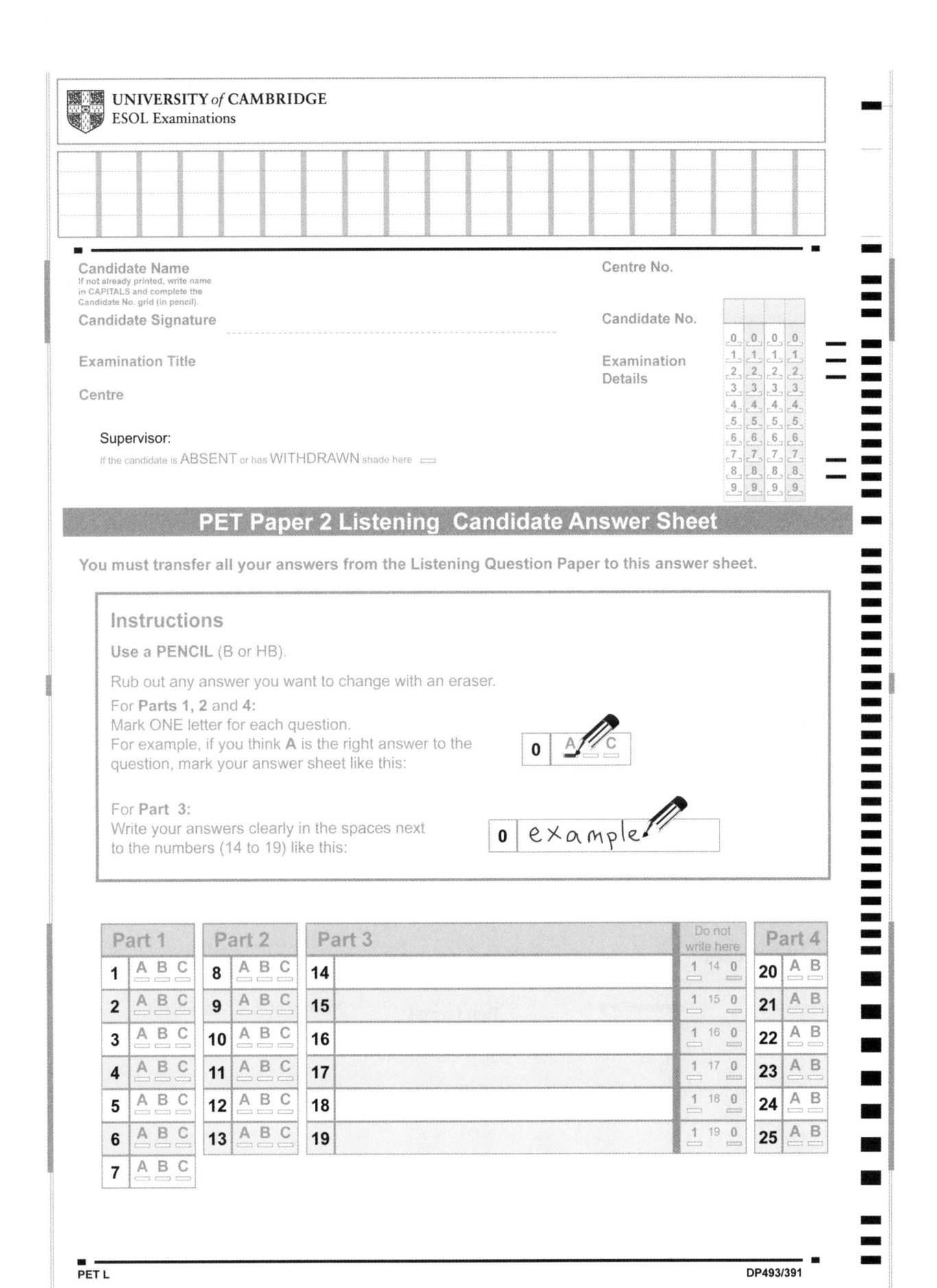

Candidate Name
If not already printed, write name in CAPITALS and complete the Candidate No. grid (in pencil).

Candidate Signature

Examination Title

Centre

Supervisor:
If the candidate is ABSENT or has WITHDRAWN shade here ▭

Centre No.

Candidate No.

Examination Details

PET Paper 2 Listening Candidate Answer Sheet

You must transfer all your answers from the Listening Question Paper to this answer sheet.

Instructions

Use a PENCIL (B or HB).

Rub out any answer you want to change with an eraser.

For **Parts 1, 2** and **4**:
Mark ONE letter for each question.
For example, if you think **A** is the right answer to the question, mark your answer sheet like this:

| 0 | A̶ C |

For **Part 3**:
Write your answers clearly in the spaces next to the numbers (14 to 19) like this:

| 0 | example |

Part 1	Part 2	Part 3	Do not write here	Part 4
1 A B C	8 A B C	14	1 14 0	20 A B
2 A B C	9 A B C	15	1 15 0	21 A B
3 A B C	10 A B C	16	1 16 0	22 A B
4 A B C	11 A B C	17	1 17 0	23 A B
5 A B C	12 A B C	18	1 18 0	24 A B
6 A B C	13 A B C	19	1 19 0	25 A B
7 A B C				

PET L   DP493/391

REPRODUCED WITH THE PERMISSION OF CAMBRIDGE ESOL © UCLES 2011   Photocopiable

UNIVERSITY of CAMBRIDGE
ESOL Examinations

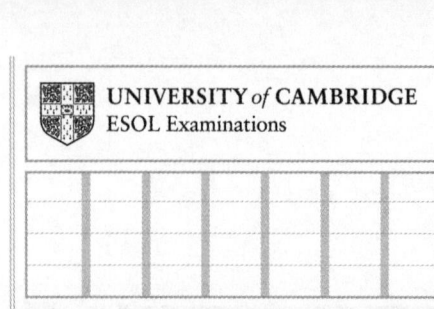

Candidate Name
If not already printed, write name in CAPITALS and complete the Candidate No. grid (in pencil).

Centre No.

Candidate No.

Examination Title

Examination Details

Centre

Supervisor:
If the candidate is ABSENT or has WITHDRAWN shade here

PET Paper 3 Speaking Mark Sheet

Date of test:

Month 01 02 03 04 05 06 07 08 09 10 11 12

Day 01 02 03 04 05 06 07 08 09 10 11 12 13 14 15 16 17 18 19 20 21 22 23 24 25 26 27 28 29 30 31

Marks awarded:

	0	1.0	1.5	2.0	2.5	3.0	3.5	4.0	4.5	5.0
Grammar and Vocabulary										
Discourse Management										
Pronunciation										
Interactive Communication										
Global Achievement										

Test materials used: 1 2 3 4 5 6 7 8 9 10

Assessor's number

Interlocutor's number

Test format

Examiners : Candidates

2 : 2

2 : 3

Number of 2nd Candidate

Number of 3rd Candidate

PET S   DP383/332

REPRODUCED WITH THE PERMISSION OF CAMBRIDGE ESOL © UCLES 2011 Photocopiable

Acknowledgements

The authors and publishers are grateful to the following for reviewing the material: Annie Broadhead; Rachel Connabeer; Laura Clyde; Rosie Ganne; Joanne Hunter; David Jay; Felicity O'Dell; Maria Sachpazian; Jessica Smith; Pauline Terzoudis; Catherine Toomey; Panagiota Tsagdi; Rosalia Valero. Many thanks also go to Sarah Salter (production controller), Michelle Simpson (permissions controller), Diane Nicholls (corpus research and analysis) and Marcus Fletcher (proof-reader)

Sue Elliott would like to give love and thanks to Dan for his IT skills, Becky and Isabelle for their infinite patience and her co-author Liz for being a great listener. Thanks also go to Ann-Marie Murphy at Cambridge University Press for all her support.

Liz Gallivan would like to give love and thanks to Roy and Max and Sue, her co-author.

Development of this publication has made use of the Cambridge International Corpus (CIC). The CIC is a computerised database of contemporary spoken and written English which currently stands at over one billion words. It includes British English, American English and other varieties of English. It also includes the Cambridge Learner Corpus, developed in collaboration with the University of Cambridge ESOL Examinations. Cambridge University Press has built up the CIC to provide evidence about language use that helps to produce better language teaching materials.

The authors and publishers acknowledge the following sources of copyright material and are grateful for the permissions granted. While every effort has been made, it has not always been possible to identify the sources of all the material used, or to trace all copyright holders. If any omissions are brought to our notice, we will be happy to include the appropriate acknowledgements on reprinting.

Solo Syndication for the text on p. 22 adapted from 'Britain's youngest airline pilot: meet the 20-year-old who flies holiday jets to the sun' by Chris Brooke, *Daily Mail* 14.1.08. Copyright © Daily Mail; Lindsay Kids of Steel for the text on p. 99 adapted from the website http://www.lindsaykidsofsteel.com/. Reproduced with permission; NI Syndication for the text on p. 100 adapted from 'James Glossop – Times Newspaper's Young Photographer of the year', *The Times* 31/7/09. Copyright © NI Syndication; The Independent for the text on p. 117 adapted from 'Teen writers show their skins' by Chris Green, *The Independent* 11.2.08. Copyright © The Independent; Text on p. 120 adapted from www.bbcnews.co.uk; The Guardian News & Media Ltd for the text on p. 153 adapted from 'I bought a long-lost Charlie Chaplin film on eBay' written by Mo Park, *The Guardian* 3.7.10 and for the text on p. 154 adapted from 'Mary-Jess Leaverland: What next for China's X Factor winner?' by Emma John, *The Observer* 20.6.10. Copyright © Guardian News & Media Ltd, 2010.

For permission to reproduce photographs:
Alamy/© Ben Molyneux People p. 014 (tc), /© Roy Wylam p. 24, /© Roberto Herrett p. 42, /© Catchlight Visual Services p. 57 (ml), /© Tetra Images p. 57 (bl), /© Ilian Animal p. 64, /© Jim Forrest p. 73 (m), /© Ladi Kirn p. 90 (ml), /© Peter Titmuss p. 90 (mr), /© Ian Shaw p. 96 (ul), /© Paul Wood p. 96 (ml), /© Wolffy p. 96 (ll), /© Emanuele Capoferri p. 99, /© Kuttig p. 114 (tl), /© Mark Baigent Life p. 114 (ul), /© Henry Beeker p. 114 (ml), /© Bubbles Photolibrary p. 117, /© John Brown p. 118, /© imagebroker p. 132 (tl), /© Johnny Greig people p. 132 (ul), /© David Young-Wolff p. 132 (ml), /© itanistock p. 132 (ll), /© MBI p. 132 (bl), /© Corbis Flirt p. 135, /© dmac p. 150 (tl), /© Dennis MacDonald p. 150 (bl), /© Corbis Bridge p. C7 (t), /© Mike Booth p. C7 (b), /© Corbis Super RF p. C9 (b), /© Indiapicture p. C10 (t), /© van hilversum p. C10 (b), /© Catchlight Visual Services p. C11 (t), /© Maurice Joseph p. C12 (b), /© image100 p. C13 (b), /© Paul Thompson Images p. C14 (b), /© MBI p. C15 (t), /© Eddie Linssen p. C15 (b), /© Ladi Kirn p. C16 (bl), /© Peter Titmuss p. C16 (br); Corbis/© Juice Images p. 15 (tl), /© Kennan Harvey/Aurora Open p. 15 (ml), /© JLP/Jose L. Pelaez p. 57 (ul), /© Michael DeYoung p. 80, /© Rick Chapman p. 96 (tl); © East News Press Agency p. 22; Fotolia/© Andy Dean p. 15 (ul); Getty/© STOCK4B p. 114 (bl), /© Blend Images/Moxie Productions p. C8 (t), /© Wilfried Krecichwost/Photodisc p. C8 (b), /© Ryuhei Shindo/Photonica p. C13 (t); © Katherine Hayes p. 100; Imagestate/© Angelo Cavalli/age fotostock p. 14 (bm), /© Howard Grey p. 48, /© Esbin-Anderson/age fotostock p. 73 (ml), /© Howard Grey p. C16 (t); iStock/© lilly3 p. 15d (ll), /© paule858 p. 61, /© Lighthousebay p. 150 (ul), /© barsik p. 150 (ml), /© greg801 p. 153, /© foto-z p. C14 (t); Photolibrary/© Sherrie Nickol p. 14 (ml), /© Reinhard Dirscherl p. 21, /© Imagesource p. 57 (ll), /© Bjorn Andren p. 96 (bl), /© Uwe Umstätter p. 114 (ll), /© Ernst Wrba p. 136, /© Photos India p. 150 (ll), /© Ron Nickel p. C11 (b), /© Chapman Wiedelphoto p. C12 (t); Rex Features/© Adrian Sherratt p. 154; Shutterstock/© Xavier Marchant p. 15 (bl), /© DenisKlimov p. 19, /© Monkey Business Images p. 57 (tl), /© NatUlrich p. C9 (t).

Commissioned photographs by Trevor Clifford at Trevor Clifford Photography: pp. 6, 44, 47, 49, 50, 86, 89.

Illustrations: Mark Draisey pp. 4, 7, 8, 9, 20, 40, 59, 69, 74, 84; Janos Jantner pp 17, 34, 36 (m, b), C1, C2, C3, C4, C5, C6; Andrew Painter pp 35, 36 (t), 37, 62, 77 (t), 106, 107, 124 (t), 142, 143, 160 (t); Bill Piggins pp 46, 71, 77 (m), 78, 79, 124 (m, b), 125, 160 (m, b), 161; Christos Skaltsas pp 29, 32, 42, 76, 82.

Audio recordings by John Green TEFL Audio. Engineer: Adam Helal; Editor: Tim Woolf; Producer: John Green. Recorded at ID Audio Studios, London.

Designed and typeset by eMC Design Ltd

Notes

Notes

Notes

Notes

Notes

Test 1 Exam practice — Speaking Part 2

Test 1 Speaking Part 2 | C1

Test 2 Exam practice — Speaking Part 2

Advice

1 Imagine what you could do with each of these to make a poster, e.g. cut pictures from the magazine, print out photos on the computer.

2 Try comparing some of the above – **I think a camera might be more useful than crayons and pens because ...**

Test 3 — Speaking Part 2

Test 4 — Speaking Part 2

Test 5

Speaking Part 2

Test 5 Speaking Part 2 | C5

Test 6 Speaking Part 2

Test 1 Exam practice — Speaking Part 3

Candidate A

Test 2 Exam practice — Speaking Part 3

Candidate A

Test 1 Exam practice — Speaking Part 3

Candidate B

Test 2 Exam practice — Speaking Part 3

Candidate B

Advice

1 In your description, think about the following: what the people are doing, where they are, what they're wearing, who you think they are, e.g. brother and sister.

2 Don't forget phrases for possibility, e.g **they might be**, **they could be**, **they must be**, **I don't think they are ...**

3 Remember to mention things that seem obvious such as clothes, colours and the weather.

Test 3 — Speaking Part 3

Candidate A

Test 4 — Speaking Part 3

Candidate A

Test 3 Speaking Part 3

Candidate B

Test 4 Speaking Part 3

Candidate B

Test 5 | Speaking Part 3

Candidate A

Test 6 | Speaking Part 3

Candidate A

Test 5 — Speaking Part 3

Candidate B

Test 6 — Speaking Part 3

Candidate B

Test 1 Speaking Part 3

Candidate C

Test 2 Speaking Part 3

Candidate C

Test 3 | Speaking Part 3

Candidate C

Test 4 | Speaking Part 3

Candidate C

C14 | Tests 3&4 Speaking Part 3

Test 5 — Speaking Part 3

Candidate C

Test 6 — Speaking Part 3

Candidate C

Test 1 Speaking Part 3

Test 2 Speaking Part 3

C16 | Tests 1&2 Speaking Part 3